The Browns Fan's
Tailgating
Guide

SPECIAL EVENT PARKING

C-4

MUNICIPAL PARKING LOT

CITY OF CLEVELAND

90-911

YOU PARK-N-LOCK YOUR OWN CAR,
THEREFORE THE CITY IS NOT
RESPONSIBLE FOR LOSS OR DAMAGE TO
PERSONAL PROPERTY LEFT IN PARKED
CARS. NOR FIRE, THEFT, COLLISION OR
OTHER DAMAGE OF THE VEHICLE.

RATES AS POSTED

The Browns Fan's Tailgating Guide

PETER CHAKERIAN

GRAY & COMPANY, PUBLISHERS
CLEVELAND

This book is dedicated Susan and Christopher.
Your love, support and encouragement is unparalleled.

Gray & Company, Publishers
www.grayco.com

Library of Congress Cataloging-in-Publication Data
Chakerian, Peter.
Browns fan's tailgating guide / Peter Chakerian.
p. cm.
ISBN 978-1-59851-045-4
1. Tailgate parties—United States. 2. Tailgate parties—United States—History. 3. Football fans—United States—Social life and customs. 4. Outdoor cookery. 5. Entertaining. 6. Cleveland Browns (Football team : 1999–) I. Title.
GV1472.C43 2008
642'.3—dc22   2008037858

ISBN: 978-1-59851-045-4

Design by Meredith Pangrace

Printed in the United States of America
First printing

"Tailgating has become a social setting, a community. On a Sunday afternoon we all want our team to win, but we're all there every week even when they don't win because we don't want to miss out on seeing our friends. It has a life of its own apart from the game and if you've never been to a tailgate before, it's almost like traveling to a foreign country. The experience goes way beyond the game itself."

—*The BoneLady, superfan from Lakewood*

"I started tailgating in the early '80s, in the days prior to the infamous 'Red Right 88' incident. Back then, it was a much simpler thing. I used to have a regular van and the group we went with would throw a picnic table in the back and some benches, and drive down to Mall C. There was some tailgating going on back then, but I have to say it wasn't nearly like it is today. There surely wasn't as much food or variety back then . . . these days people go all out."

—*Tony "Mobile Dawg" Schaefer,*
superfan from Sandusky

"Up until last season, the Browns have been painful to watch. In the previous four years, we've gone 5-11, 4-12, 6-10 and 4-12 . . . With a record like that, you need a good party!"

—*Josh Donald, Lakewood*

CONTENTS

The Browns Fan's
Tailgating
Guide

INTRODUCTION

It's just before dawn on Sunday morning in late November.
The streetlights that stand guard along East 9th Street in
downtown Cleveland are still buzzing and casting their eerie
glow on the asphalt below. It's the only sound you hear walking north toward Lake Erie—except for maybe the lake itself.
Sunrise is still a ways off and most people are still in bed or,
at the very least, taking their first bleary-eyed sips of coffee
with the morning paper.

But not you. With each block walked, a new sound touch-
es your ears. People. Music. Laughter. A sports radio talk
show host speculating from a radio's speakers. Chanting and
cheering. Then come the smells. Burgers. Sausages. Breakfast and barbecue. Wood fires. You feel your pulse begin to
quicken.

As you walk down East 9th, the illuminated Cleveland
Browns Stadium billboard intermittently brightens your
path. Once past the North Coast Garage, you head east on
the south sidewalk running parallel to the Shoreway. You
look up and see some people stirring by their vehicles in the
garage. They're pulling out lawn chairs, grills and coolers
and listening to the latest news on the Cleveland Browns.
And a couple of minutes later, you're standing in the Cleveland Municipal ("Muni") Parking Lot with a whole host of
Browns fans.

You glance at your watch. A little after 5 a.m. Campfires

crackle and football jersey-clad friends and family are shaking out the cobwebs with laughter and merriment. Tents and tables are getting set up. And before you even think to ask anyone, you overhear the first group your eyes focus on. A group of twelve is hanging a banner between trees and talking over breakfast at their campsite.

Taking *their* first bleary-eyed sips of coffee—or whatever that might be in those coffee mugs they're sporting—they share the morning paper, too. They ask each other how they slept—in the vehicles parked next to them . . . in this very parking lot. They've been there since late Saturday afternoon.

Welcome to Cleveland Browns Tailgating

Joe Cahn, the cheerful former owner of the New Orleans School of Cooking and self-proclaimed "Commissioner of Tailgating," calls the modern day tailgating phenomenon found before sporting events "The Last Great American Neighborhood" and "The Last Great American Pastime."

He should know: he has spent the last decade of his life traveling across the country, searching for that next great tailgate experience. His taglines for tailgating are fitting, and yet they don't even begin to scratch the surface in describing the parties you'll find in a *hardcore* football town like Cleveland.

Like fans in other gridiron strongholds in the Midwest, Clevelanders love tailgating almost as much as the beloved Browns team they honor with their parties every week. Tailgating is more than just a get-together packed with like-minded football enthusiasts, it's an *event*—a weekly opportunity for creativity and camaraderie to spring eternal alongside the hopes we all have for the team's success. And tailgating isn't just big in Cleveland, it is big everywhere.

Some tailgating lives up to the questionable reputation it has earned over the years. It won't take a new bystander long to see that there's some hardcore revelry and excess going on every Sunday—the kind usually reserved for the likes of college freshmen free of their parents. But there's also a kinder, gentler and larger shared experience that borders on collective consciousness.

Tailgating is one of the few homespun, grassroots "happenings" still amazingly unspoiled by corporate America. Despite its popularity and surging tailgate-related sales reaching $12 *billion* in 2007, the experience is still largely owned and operated by fans. Which is how it should always be. And no one does tailgating better than football towns like Cleveland.

A pastime unto itself, tailgating draws from dozens of inspirations. A Browns tailgate is equal parts Bourbon Street Mardi Gras party, big-top circus, custom car/RV show, huge, zoo-like Ohio University Halloween party, costume ball, fraternity party, camping trip, gourmet cooking competition, rock concert, fashion show, festival, picnic, "wedding reception on steroids" and family reunion rolled into one.

From the three-ring circus that is the Cleveland Municipal "Muni" Parking Lot, to the other pockets of parking situated all around Cleveland Browns Stadium, pregame tailgating brings out unparalleled energy and enthusiasm in the variety of fans who attend. And like the fans themselves, each parking lot has a completely different personality from the other . . . except perhaps for the Muni Lot, which has something of a multiple personality complex.

"Cleveland fans are a legion of Charlie Browns," says writer Greg Deegan in his recent book *Surviving the Drought.* And since 1964, fans of the Browns have had a host of Lucys pull the football away just as they were set to kick it through the uprights. But that doesn't mean that the fans party like the Peanuts gang at Thanksgiving—feasting on buttered toast, pretzels, popcorn, jelly beans and ice cream sundaes—before the big game. Not on your life.

We might well be a legion of Charlie Browns, but we can surely throw a great Sunday party and know one when we see it. Tailgaters across the country are serious about their parties, spending an average of $250 per person annually on the pursuit. Browse the lakefront before a home game and you'll see that Browns fans at least meet that average, if not exceed it. And Browns fans *always* do it up right, regardless of what the scoreboard says during the year.

Each season, the number of Browns tailgaters increases. Their campsites in the parking lots get more complex and decidedly high tech every season, replete with high definition television sets, satellite dishes, gas-powered blenders and gigantic, customized grills and smokers—you know, the kind that accommodate pig roasts and sides of beef. It all brings to mind those colossal brontosaurus ribs from *The Flintstones* that used to tip Fred's car over after every episode.

The quality of feasting and beverages far outshines the early burgers, brats, beer and crudités approach that's synonymous with tailgating. You're likely to see fans scarfing down everything from beer-battered macaroni and cheese to sauerkraut balls, wings and poppers. Others are deep-frying turkeys, breaking out homemade pots of savory jambalaya and clam chowder, comparing their own homebrewed beers and uncovering flank steaks, pulled pork, chicken skewers and lobster bakes.

If your mind can dream up the perfect meal, you're guaranteed to find it while trolling the lots on a Sunday. The only thing missing is the fancy white tablecloth.

But more than the quality of the food, the wealth of gear and the obsessive and meticulous preparation, tailgating is all about the people who make up the experience. Everyone looks out for each other. Your "neighbors" go missing from their usual spots in the lot on a given Sunday and fellow tailgaters are quick to the cell phone with a call wondering why.

There is a kinship, caste system or social organization to tailgating. Some longtime tailgaters have parked in the same place for a decade or longer and set up their own "neighborhood watch" to make sure those time-honored places are reserved for the right fans on a Sunday. And yet, all of the things that divide us as citizens—race, ethnicity, gender, creed, age, social status—get put on hold for a while when people come together as tailgating fans. Unless you're from an AFC North rival city sporting your gear, that is. But we'll get to that later on in the book.

When a new group treads on another's "reserved" space—or gets carried away with their PG-13 fun or R-rated celebrating—all of the neighbors go out of their way to police the turf, just like neighborhoods of old. No one wants an altercation with law enforcement, or for the party to be shut down before its time. As a result, everyone protects those around them from jeopardizing a "Dawg Day Afternoon" at what's been called "Cleveland's family picnic."

In keeping with that neighborhood analogy, most tailgaters will share a beer or a meal with their neighbors in the same way one might borrow a cup of sugar from a neighbor back in the good old days. Generosity is the call for the day; some Browns tailgaters bring enough food to feed the homeless citizens who wander to the lots for a diversion and sustenance. In that sense, tailgating transcends all of the descriptions previously offered and becomes a microcosm of society. It's a pop culture phenomenon for sure, but it's not a stretch to liken this outdoor dining and party experience to cultural anthropology.

Browns fans are among the most diehard, bighearted, passionate and *creative* people there are in Northeast Ohio. They are also among the heartiest NFL tailgaters in the country; they come out rain or shine, when it's eighty above or twenty below with the wind chill, playoff bound, or merely angling for the best possible draft choice.

They open their camps to new friends, share meals with the less fortunate and channel all the creativity they usually stuff down during the week into the weekends. To paraphrase the old saying, Browns tailgaters party like they don't need money, love the Browns like they've never been hurt, and create a spectacle like no one's watching. They know how to live.

The lots and stadium seats are almost always full. In August and September, you'll have some "fair weather" fans— people who come out when weather is beautiful, then retreat to their TV rooms as the temperature drops. But when the temperature dips, you find resolute Browns fans with their core convictions intact: they're gritty, frozen, dogged and absolutely obsessive about the party and the team. And that says nothing of those "Training Camp" tailgaters who turn up and party at the Browns training facility in Berea before the kids are back in school.

Hundreds of Browns fans were observed and consulted, mostly on background, in the writing of this book. The vast majority of information comes from my own personal interviews, experiences with (and interpretation of) Browns tailgaters, all of whom were charitable with their time, food, provisions and insights. I'd need another whole book just to thank them all individually.

A number of tailgating stories, news features, books, online resources and the team's Web site, as well as the Cleveland Browns media guide round out the finer points and research for this all-purpose book.

This guidebook is not intended to explicitly direct a Browns tailgater's first experience or perfectly frame the longtime Browns tailgater's years of history in the lots. Rather, I hope that it serves as a good jumping-off point and conversation piece for each group of people, respectively. I hope it provides a fun, enthusiastic and commemorative record filled with past and present day experiences, tailgate stories and an inspiration to join the tailgating ranks this season and beyond.

Please enjoy the *Browns Fan's Tailgating Guide* and the traditions that run parallel to Cleveland Browns football. I hope it inspires you to create or enhance your own Browns tailgating experience on game day. Go Browns!

Layne Anderson

ORIGIN AND HISTORY OF CLEVELAND BROWNS TAILGATING

A Tailgating Genesis

At the dawn of the Automotive Age, the word "tailgate" referred specifically to the hinged back section of a vehicle that could be removed or let up or down for the ease in loading or unloading cargo. Although its invention was a convenience for the driver and passengers, it's become the foundation for the modern tailgating experience that has come to accompany concerts and sporting events.

When did the concept of "tailgating" start? Some say that the very first college football game between Rutgers and Princeton back in 1869 served as the very first tailgating experience. Back then, spectators traveled to the game by horse-drawn carriages, and spent the time prior to kickoff grilling sausages and burgers at the "tail end" of the horse.

Others suggest that the phenomenon began at Yale University in 1904. By all accounts, a locomotive made up of private railcars had transported a throng of fans to a Yale football game. When that train stopped at the station—a fair distance from the stadium, according to the story—the fans inside were starving. From there the idea was hatched by the fans to bring along appropriate provisions to be consumed before the start of the next game.

Still others claim that the cradle of tailgating is Green Bay, Wisconsin, and point to the year 1919, when the three-time Super Bowl Champion Green Bay Packers were first formed. Wisconsin farmers would back their pickup trucks around the edge of the open football field, open their tailgates to sit on and graze from a picnic basket of food as they watched "The Pack" play.

Freelance writer Chris Warner, who wrote *A Tailgater's Guide To SEC Football*, produced a 2003 documentary on tailgating for The History Channel cable network's *Modern Marvels* series. In it, Warner suggests any of the three origins could be considered valid, but that "[W]hile modern tailgating has only recently [within the last 30 years] become popular, the practice of enjoying both food and football has post-Civil War, 19th century roots."

Origins of Cleveland Browns Tailgating

Depending on which Browns fans you talk to, you're likely to get a number of different answers on when pregame Browns tailgating began. Some will tell you that 1964 Championship was a watershed moment for tailgating, but those people have difficulty pointing you to someone who actually experienced it first-hand during those days. Others point to the September 1970 *Monday Night Football* premiere of the Browns against the New York Jets as the beginning of the tailgating phenomenon here in Cleveland.

In both cases, the idea of "tailgating" was probably a far cry from the experience it is today. It was more like a brown-bag lunch or picnic basket with a little something extra before game time. Author, NPR commentator and longtime Cleveland Browns fan Scott Huler sums up what he calls "pre-tailgating times" on the North Coast (pre-late '70s):

> "Our tailgating consisted of making pastrami sandwiches with brown mustard on Kaiser rolls, putting them in baggies with napkins and little baggies of potato chips, and bringing them to the Stadium with us [and] also a thermos of coffee [or] a little flask of 'tea,' but again: no actual tailgating." —*Scott Huler, author and Cleveland expatriate living in Raleigh, N.C.*

If you're to believe most tailgaters, festivities before Browns games never really hit their stride until the 1980s—first with Sam Rutigliano's "Kardiac Kids" success, and then with the AFC Championship teams helmed by the team's beloved quarterback, Bernie Kosar. That's when a few lakefront fan photos begin to emerge in local print media.

But do a little more digging and you'll find that the spirit and atmosphere on the lakefront before the big game might owe a debt to an almost completely unrelated event on the same premises.

In 2007, tailgating was cited as a $12 billion a year industry. As many as 51 million Americans were expected to participate in tailgating that year. The number of tailgating Americans has been rising steadily (roughly 12 percent annually) over the last five years, according to the American Tailgating Association (ATA). This $12 billion figure statistic is staggering when one considers the National Football League generates approximately $7 billion in annual revenue.

Long Before the Tailgate Party on the North Coast

Cleveland's lakefront landscape has changed a great deal over the years, but one thing has remained constant: Cleveland football (both Rams and Browns) has taken place on the lakefront as long as most football fans can remember. Cleveland Municipal Stadium, which opened July 1, 1931, served as the home of Browns fans for generations until its demolition in November 1996. (Aside from football, the venue played host to everything from boxing matches and baseball to concert events.)

The area *surrounding* that F.R. Walker-designed Municipal Stadium has had a rather festive history, playing host to the grand Great Lakes Exposition in the mid-1930s as a centennial celebration of Cleveland's incorporation. The exposition was a huge to-do—not to mention a welcome respite for Clevelanders enduring the Great Depression.

The exposition was a great place for a picnicking, shopping, live music and entertainment for millions of residents during its two-year lakefront tenure. Stretching as far south as Public Hall and east to where today's Cleveland State Uni-

Where it all began: Cleveland Municipal Stadium. *(Cleveland Public Library Archives)*

Long before the party: East Ninth Street during the Great Lakes Exposition in the mid-1930s. *(Cleveland State University Archives)*

versity begins, the exposition featured jazz and dance concerts, parties, a floating stage and, at the north end/mouth of East 9th Street, a magnificent entryway that ushered in patrons.

The core "footprint" for the exposition's fairgrounds reflects most of the Browns tailgating locations there are to choose from today, including the ground occupied by the Great Lakes Science Center, the Rock and Roll Hall of Fame, Burke Lakefront Airport and the remaining land on either side of today's North and South Marginal Roads that makes up the now legendary Cleveland Municipal Parking (known as "Muni") Lot.

From the Heyday to the Move . . . and Back

From the 1980s on, the Browns experienced a surge, popularity and heyday not seen since the '64 Championship. And the fans set about to celebrate the return to form in the many key tailgating locations that Browns fans still have to choose from.

The Muni Lot; the Burke Lakefront Airport and adjacent Naval Lot; the northernmost Port Authority Lot (now called the "Yellow Lot"); parking lots to the west of the stadium off of West 3rd Street, near the Route 2 overpass (sometimes referred to as "The Pit"); and down into the East Bank of the Flats all have faithfully served as bastions for Cleveland tailgaters and continue to draw the most revelers. Other locations off of East 9th Street; the Justice Center and Lakeside Avenue Parking; Mall B/C by the Convention Center, and the Warehouse District tended to draw fans who were headed to a busy tailgate location, directly to the stadium or to brunching and barhopping for the game.

Sadly, many of these party parking locations went silent during the 1996 NFL season, after Browns owner Art Modell had moved the team to Baltimore. It would be a heartbreaking three years of disorder, resentment and, for some people, regular commutes to Buffalo, New York for Bills "Browns Day" games and to Columbus for Ohio State Buckeyes games before a tailgating Browns fan's life would return to normal. Some tailgating fans were so lost without the Browns, they "couldn't even stomach watching football," choosing instead to drown themselves in home projects, golf and a variety of other sports to occupy their time.

When the Browns finally returned in 1999, all of these locations were beyond invigorated, filled with old and new generations of fans. Today, tailgating before a Browns game is more popular than ever. Tens of thousands of fans jam all of these downtown locations to tailgate before each home game. And not all of these fans have tickets for the game. Some of them spend the *entire game* in the lot, or head to their favorite local watering hole when the crowds start their approach to the stadium. Some of these tailgate locations are low-key and laid back; others are nothing less than a carnival midway.

Today's Browns Tailgating Lots

The Best of the Best: The Muni Lot

To say that the Muni Lot offers the best of the best in Cleveland tailgating is an understatement. Browns fans who travel to games will tell you that few NFL cities can rival the enthusiasm found at the East 9th Street and South Marginal Road tailgate. Fans who have experienced other hardcore NFL tailgating cities (Green Bay, Chicago and Kansas City among them) say that our very own Muni Lot celebration can hang with them all.

"Oh, the humanity!" A bird's eye view of the Muni from the North Coast Garage deck. *(Layne Anderson)*

Where the magic happens: the Muni Lot Entrance. Parking spot in 2007: $15. Soaking up the biggest circus in Cleveland? Priceless. *(Layne Anderson)*

The 2007 *Sports Illustrated* "NFL Fan Value Experience" confirms this to a large degree. *Sports Illustrated* editors sifted through over 17,000 responses to an online survey that evaluated NFL stadiums. And as one might expect, tailgating was a critical component. Only two stadiums—Lambeau Field in Green Bay and Heinz Field in Pittsburgh (*boo!*)—earned higher marks than the Browns' home turf.

Cleveland earned 6 out of a possible 10-point score for the tailgating category, yet the city finished a stellar third place overall for game day atmosphere—due in large part (one has to believe) to the euphoria found in downtown parking lots, including the mighty Muni.

The Muni Lot is a melting pot of Browns fans and it looks and feels like a big top circus in spots. The diversity of cultures, social classes, ages and ethnic backgrounds is unmatched among game day parking lot choices that Browns fans have. It's not a stretch to call the Muni Lot a city unto itself, as one longtime Cleveland broadcaster and another longtime Cleveland sports reporter reflect:

> "It's Munitown! It's a city, a town and a village, you know? The Muni Lot is a compassionate, sharing village with an abundance of everything. It's a little Cleveland: you have everyone from blue-collar to white-collar, line workers to entrepreneurs and all points in between. You have your small scale groups with little Weber grills to giant parties with deluxe gas grills, campsites, fire pits and truckloads of firewood, and a ton of great food. What's amazing to me is just how many people treat it like a second home and a rite of passage. And there's a tradition and magnitude there from September to December that's almost as staunch as wearing a bonnet on Easter used to be back in the day." —*Mark "Munch" Bishop, sports talk show host, WKNR 850 AM*

"I think what you see down there is indicative of the true Browns fan—they'll wake up early and commit a lot of time to what they do. It's not just a football game for them, and even after starting that early, the fans will go back to the Muni Lot and spend a couple more hours after that waiting for the traffic to lighten. That's a full eight to nine hours of party-ing. It's remarkable, too, because there hasn't been a lot to cheer about until recently. It is one thing to party for and cheer on a team that's winning, but that's not as easy to do when the team has been in the doldrums for so long. To finally reward those people with a good team is a long time coming."
— *Tony Grossi,* **Plain Dealer** *Browns beat reporter*

The environment in the Muni Lot tends to draw a lot of the members of the media, all with the idea of covering the pre-game festivities. Fans will find their share of camera crews trolling the lot for both local *and* national media—filming and broadcasting comments from boisterous and excited fans. It's not for everyone, as WJW-TV 8 News sports reporter Dan Coughlin recalls during his "first and last" experience in the Muni Lot:

"I'll be honest, I haven't covered a whole lot of tail-gating in my career. And I can't say that I would rec-ommend it based on the one experience that I had. Back in 1999 when the Browns came back, a cam-eraman and I agreed to shoot a piece down in the Muni Lot. And from where we were standing, it was like walking into a bar at midnight when everyone is drunk and you're the only one sober. Our camera seemed to attract [all of them]. It was a zoo, and the cameraman and I agreed we'd never do it again. It was just not for me."
— *Dan Coughlin, WJW-TV 8 sports anchor*

A vintage shot of Browns tailgating in the Muni Lot, circa 1980. *(Cleveland State University Archives)*

It's not really all "heathens and animals" as one fan put it last year, but Coughlin's experience can be a common one—especially for the uninitiated. Starting your tailgating experience in the Muni Lot is like diving into the deep end of the swimming pool without sticking your toe in first. It can be an all-or-nothing fan pride proposition and the people and activities there can often get quite rowdy. But don't let that discourage you: the camps of like-minded Muni fans tend to gravitate toward one another, which creates a number of "mood zones" there. Television crews tend to draw out that rowdy behavior, especially during AFC North rivalry games, in the Muni Lot.

"Tailgating in the Muni Lot, at least in some parts of it, can be age-appropriate. There's this illusion that somehow all tailgaters are low-income, irresponsible, non-professional, beer-drinking jerks. And the fact of the matter is that most of us are anything but that. When you go to a regular party, sometimes the people there can be stiff. When you go to a Browns tailgate, everyone has a common bond, love is in the air. I would say the phenomenon of how nice people are in general is what I'd want people to know about Browns tailgating. I've seen some things get out of hand and seen things go positively. It's all good. Tailgating is a phenomenon that you just don't get watching on TV. When the cameras are on, it can all seem a little crazy, but it's like Mardi Gras: you have to be there to appreciate it. It's a mini Mardi Gras for every game." —***The Taj, superfan from Hudson***

To paraphrase the Las Vegas tourism board, what happens in the Muni Lot *stays* in the Muni Lot. The Muni Lot is the game day epicenter for Browns tailgaters. Fans arrive at the crack of dawn—some even camping out overnight there—all to ensure that regular tailgate spots are maintained. There's a loose caste and rule system that is imposed by regulars in the lot to make sure that "reserved" parking spots for longtime tailgaters aren't taken by others. That passion the fans have for Muni Lot Browns celebrations have actually influenced one local sportscaster to anchor his Sunday morning pregame broadcasts there:

"When we were deciding where to do our WKNR Browns pregame show, being a proud Clevelander— and a Slavic Village and Harvard/Lee kid—I knew there was nowhere else we could possibly be on a Sunday. That's where we needed to be . . . I mean, how could we not be down there? Everyone at the station jumped at the idea, which was great. And

now that we're down at the Muni, there's a steady
stream of people who stop in while I'm broadcasting down there. The pride you see from all of them
is pretty incredible: people bring over their sons,
daughters, their dads, new wives. It's all pretty cool."
—***Mark "Munch" Bishop***

Aside from being the main lot for tailgating in Cleveland,
the Muni Lot is also quite unique to the NFL—it is a parking
lot owned by the City of Cleveland, not by the home team,
as is the case in other popular NFL tailgating cities. This apparently led to concerns regarding the legal responsibility of
tailgate activities for the city. Former Mayor Jane Campbell
may have been the most outspoken opponent of celebrations there, and most people in the Muni Lot will tell you
this didn't exactly endear her to tailgaters who call it home
on Sundays:

"I remember hearing . . . a couple people were
hurt pretty bad with fireworks at a tailgate and that
the city was worried about being sued because
they own the lot. It could have gotten nasty, but I
think that's what led to all the police being down
there. Honestly, having the cops are down there is
great. We always tell people to just have fun, and
cooperate. If [Mayor Campbell] had shut [the Muni

Tailgaters spend $250 per person annually,
according to the American Tailgating Association (ATA). Their
2007 research survey also indicated 57 percent of tailgaters earn
at least $75,000 annually; 82 percent are homeowners and 41
percent said that they spend more than $500 per
season on food and other tailgating provisions. Now that's a lot
of burgers, brats and beer.

Lot tailgating] down, I don't know what would have happened. I don't think [she] would have been able to stop it. Tailgating is so in the blood of people down there that if anyone tried to shut everything down, they would have had to arrest the whole Muni Lot." *—Tony "Mobile Dawg" Schaefer, superfan and tailgater, Sandusky*

After a couple of hot-tempered situations in the lot, Campbell threatened to shut down the Muni Lot parties altogether. Her fears suggested that the circus-like atmosphere would lead to greater widespread trouble and lawlessness. Her plan was ultimately abandoned in favor of placing regular police on shifts there to maintain the peace. Campbell also surrounded the entire lot with chain link fencing to keep overzealous fans off of the Shoreway to the north and the train/RTA rapid transit tracks to the south:

"I think that whole Jane Campbell thing got a little ridiculous, really. [Her plan] came about after a beer throwing incident during a game inside the stadium. The officials screwed up a play, I think during the Kansas City Chiefs game [in 2003]. There was a lot of beer throwing in the stadium that day and after that, there was a push to stop all partying and grilling in the Muni Lot—like somehow the beer being consumed in the Muni Lot had more to do with it than the same beer sold in the stadium. It was all kind of bizarre and before I knew it, I was on the radio on WMMS, and on TV and was pushed to the forefront talking about 'Queen Jane' on what my feelings were on the subject. She never shut anything down over there, which was a good thing. But she did build that fence to keep people contained. You can see what that got her around election time! I guess she can adopt the Muni Lot as her legacy." *—The Taj*

Today, the Muni Lot maintains the most delicate relationship between fans and law enforcement in all of the National
Football League. Dealing with a diverse array of potentially
hazardous situations—open alcohol containers, fire pits,
the occasionally hostile and violent fan, etc.—most of the
Lot's "neighbors" work hard to police themselves. Everyone
makes sure there's not a reason for the Cleveland Police
to get actively involved in an altercation. The respect Muni
Lot tailgaters have for the police presence is a big deal and
clearly a positive thing:

> "People really care about each other down there,
> whether you're a hometown fan or not. Even with
> Steelers fans . . . [they] might get the whole 'Pitts-
> burgh Sucks' chant as they walk by in their gear, but
> you also see them get pulled aside by the Browns
> fans and offered something to eat or drink, too. It's
> all done with sportsmanship. Yes, you get some
> village idiots. Every week, there's one or two of
> those—every city has them—adding that touch of
> anarchy or mischief to the order. But mostly, it's a re-
> spectful experience and most of the time, the police
> you see down there working the lot are being treated
> almost like family." *—Mark "Munch" Bishop*

> "Tailgating, at least in the Muni Lot, is age appropri-
> ate. Come early, be responsible, party hard, enjoy
> the game and go home. If you're a Browns fan,
> that's what you should do. Come on ahead. If you
> want to discuss the game and your 401(k) retirement
> account, come to the stadium ten minutes before
> game time, have a couple drinks while you're there,
> then find a bar somewhere afterward." *—The Taj*

The Best of the Rest

There are literally dozens of tailgating pockets spread out all across the lakefront on any given Browns Sunday. Each one of them has its own unique personality and draws crowds that are appropriate to that vibe:

Next to the Muni Lot sits the **North Coast Garage**. Although not a true tailgating "destination," this multi-tiered, concrete parking deck serves as a home base and overflow parking for some Muni Lot regulars—most of whom use the space for shelter for themselves and their cars when the weather turns severe. This parking deck tends to fill up by 10:30 a.m., long after the Muni is at or near capacity. And while you're not likely to see anything compared to the Muni happening in there from top to bottom, some fans do line up along the north and east facings of the structure to party and survey the other parties. It's the best tailgating location for people watchers.

It's not as sexy as the Muni Lot, but you'll still find a few diehard partiers in that North Coast garage, surveying the Muni Lot landscape and using the parking deck as their home base. You can meet a fair number of "Tailgate No-mads" there—people who don't set up a Muni Lot camp themselves—during most home games. If you don't have a regular group to tailgate with, connecting with these people and bouncing from camp to camp and lot to lot can be a real blast. Leave the car, strap on a backpack full of cold beverages, and stop in at several locations before game time. It can be a blast. You can cover a lot of ground that way and make new friends in the process. Just be sure to wear some comfortable shoes.

Across the Shoreway from the Muni Lot and North Coast sits both the **Burke Lakefront Airport Lot** and the **Naval Lot**. Both of these locations are nearly adjacent to each other and sit across the street from the Rock and Roll Hall of Fame and Museum at the end of East 9th Street on North Marginal

Left: The Port Lot used to be a tailgating haven in the old Municipal Stadium days. Back then, hibachis were the big thing. *(Cleveland Public Library Archives)*

Below: Ask this clan where the real fun is on Sundays for tailgating. They (and others) will tell you the Burke/Naval Lots are tops with families who prefer a slightly less manic (but no less passionate) alternative to what's across the Shoreway at the Muni Lot. *(Layne Anderson)*

Below: Back in the day, tailgaters didn't have nearly as much gear—but that didn't keep them from partying and hunkering down in the many lots. *(Cleveland Public Library Archives)*

Road. These two lots offer a much tamer, lower-key version of the Muni Lot. And for those looking for a little more, shall we say, *privacy*, the Burke lot has full-fledged, accessible restrooms instead of the scattered port-a-potties (and worse) at Muni.

Expect to see the same wide range of custom vehicles, canopies, grilling stations and creativity in the Burke and Naval lots, but with a little less explosive energy. Those who party there still have a blast, but it's a bit more relaxed affair.

> "We've been going down sporadically since the mid-1980s and used to bounce around between lots back in the old Municipal Stadium days, but after the new Browns stadium was built, we were parked predominately at the Burke Lakefront [Airport]. It's always a lot of fun, and usually pretty busy and hopping. But we ended up in the Muni Lot because we'd be sitting there watching all of these people across the Shoreway having a great time."
> **—John Schoger, Lakewood**

To the west of the Rock Hall, the **Great Lakes Science Center Lot** and **Port Authority ("Yellow") Lot** tend to have some tailgating in them, but in a much different and more refined way. Season ticket holders, stadium workers, Browns players and those people lucky enough to have media credentials during the season tend to centralize in those two lots. As a result, the vibe is decidedly lighter, more family-friendly and even a bit more formal than the other locations. Not all of the people who park there tailgate, but even those who don't still have great appreciation for the environment there:

> "The thing I've always noticed walking through the [Yellow] Port Authority Lot is that oftentimes there are at least two or three generations of fans out there,

grilling brats, wearing jerseys from different eras and generally enjoying themselves. And for all the discussion of sloppy, down-in-the-mud drunk tailgating behavior, more often than not, they're all sipping coffee, cocoa or soda pop and throwing the football around. It's a family experience, and a real binding experience." —**Terry Pluto,** **Plain Dealer** *sports columnist*

"I don't get anywhere near the Muni Lot because it's not near where I need to be—members of the media park in the Port Lot north of the stadium. There are always a lot of fans tailgating there. I am sure those are folks have the prime club seats. It looks like they have a lot of fun. There have been times where I'd have rather been with them than covering the game." —**Tony Grossi**

These two spots, along with the **Route 2 Bridge Underpass** (which is **also known as "The Pit"**) and **down into the West Bank of the Flats**, seem to attract a slightly more sophisticated group of tailgaters who might find the other lots overwhelming. This area is where you find the Old Schoolers. It's not cliquey or elitist, but don't plan to hang out there if you've got a Muni Lot mindset. If you're looking for some seasoned, independent-minded tailgaters who have been around the block a time or two, then this location is for you. The people there go all out with their food and fun, but tend to take in the day with an "act like you've been there" mentality. It's definitely a contrast to the Muni Lot frat party.

"When I got out of school in 1976, I started tailgating with some of my brother's buddies down there. We've been down there ever since—never even entertained another place. I've been down there since we started tailgating and I wouldn't go anywhere else. The Pit is a much more family-oriented location than some of the others. Week after week, you're seeing the same people, passing along beers amongst each other; the kids are throwing the football and playing cornhole now. Even cigar smells get the guys talking . . . There's a lot going on down there. Sometimes, I just walk around the area and check out what the vendors have, and visit some friends that you find in the same spots all the time. [Browns punter] Dave Zastudil's buddies and friends are all in The Pit." —*Jim Sgro, Parma*

"We've been going down to tailgate for Browns games since the team came back in 1999. We have found that the area at West 3rd and Summit is really a great family lot. Everyone brings their kids down there; it doesn't get as rowdy as some of the other lots do. Everyone gets down there early, around 7 a.m., and most of us hang out there all day, even long after the game is over. I went with a couple of buddies at first, and then my wife and son started coming." —*Bob Geiger, Bay Village*

West of the stadium, there are several other locations to park. **Dock 20 ("Blue Lot"), Dock 32, Canal Basin** and spots in the **Warehouse District** tend to be hit or miss. Same goes for **Voinovich Park** and **Willard Park Garage** on East 9th Street, which serve as overflow for fans of both the Muni and Burke/Naval Lot tailgate parties. Tailgating is prohibited in these

Statistics show that more than 30 million people tailgate at least once in a typical football season (be it NCAA or NFL). It's becoming one of the fastest growing recreational activities in the country.

You won't get a toast like *this* at your ordinary local bar. (Layne Anderson)

locations; yet, some very small groups will still settle into these spots to avoid the bustle and rowdy crowds. If they keep a low profile, usually these people are left to their own devices.

Parking at the **Justice Center**, the **Galleria**, and locations spread out along **Lakeside Avenue** are strictly for parking only—no tailgating is allowed and it's a rule that's enforced. Back in the day (read: the 1980s) tailgaters used to use Malls B and C as regular tailgating locations. You'll still find a few rogues camped out in the latter-mentioned area and spread as far south as the Louis Stokes Wing of the Cleveland Public Library off Superior.

For the Tailgate Nomad

You might be the type of person who loves the idea of tailgating, but might not have a large group to tailgate with. Outside of joining a network like the Cleveland Browns Backers or one of the many online Browns communities, you might just strap the party to your back and head to one of the tailgating locations that sounds appealing to you. Being a "Tailgate Nomad" can also be rather inexpensive—outside of paying to park or taking public transportation, having some decent beverages or other treats to barter/share is a great icebreaker to help you connect with some established tailgaters.

> "I get a lot of invitations to join a tailgate [in] the different lots every week, so I really end up being more of a nomad than anything. I go down and park my car somewhere, make my way to a location and stay there for a while. Then I move on to the next place."
> —*Wayne Lett, Browns 24/7 editor, Conneaut*

If becoming a "Tailgate Nomad" sounds interesting to you, consider the Greater Cleveland Regional Transit Authority (RTA) as your cheapest and best transportation solution.

With RTA, many of the bus lines (and all of the rapid transit train lines) include or end at Tower City Center, and allow for easy transfer to the RTA Waterfront Line rapid transit. You can also access the Muni Lot, the North Coast station (near the Willard Park and North Coast garages) and west bank of the Flats with the RTA Waterfront Line rapid transit. Information for these and other public transportation options can be obtained by calling RTA at 216-621-9500, or by visiting their Web site at www.rideRTA.com. You can also buy RTA multi-trip passes and farecards on that site.

Plot out your potential lot options by using MapQuest and using the Cleveland Browns Stadium street address (100 Alfred Lerner Way, Cleveland 44114) as your destination point. Mapquest can be found online at www.mapquest.com.

Barstoolgating

Whether you're a Tailgate Nomad, a hardcore tailgater, or someone in between without tickets or an option that allows you to watch the Browns game, your best bet is to connect with someone near you and watch the game in the lot you're in. Many tailgaters have elaborate television set-ups—complete with high-definition plasma screens and portable satellite dish rigs. We'll talk about those entertainment systems in a later chapter.

Barring that approach, there are a number of great watering holes and restaurants within striking distance of Cleveland Browns Stadium and the tailgate lots listed earlier. These locations fill up fast, but offer fans a chance to watch the game if going to/staying in the lot is just not an option. They also make great postgame stops:

Alesci's Cleveland
828 Huron Rd. E. / 216-348-8600
www.alescis.com
Casual homemade Italian food there is authentic, inexpensive and no-frills. Clevelanders familiar with the Alesci's (market) name can attest to hearty portions, deli sandwiches, and great chicken parmesan. Alesci's offers $2 Miller Lite pints and drink specials on game day.

Blind Pig Speakeasy
1228 West 6th St. / 216-621-0001
www.theblindpig.com
A friendly, but chaotic location that recalls a mid-range college bar. With great pub food and enough TVs to fill your average Best Buy or Circuit City, Blind Pig (and the attached Dive Bar) is the official home of the Young OSU Buckeyes of Greater Cleveland.

Bob Golic's Sports Bar & Grille
1213 West 6th St.
The former Browns nose tackle is the latest tenant at the corner of West 6th and Lakeside Avenue, in the former Synergy nightclub space. Golic currently hosts a radio show on Akron-based WNIR 100.1 FM, and his space is said to draw

inspiration from broadcasting legend Harry Caray's restaurant in Chicago.

Boneyard Beer Farm
746 Prospect Ave. / 216-575-0226
www.boneyardusa.com
Perfect for the beer snob. Almost always packed (get there early), this is a popular stop for young professionals. They have forty-eight different cold brews on draft and the NFL Network pumped in on plasma TVs so you can follow other teams in action. Great salads for dieters and the weight conscious.

Cleats Gateway
2123 East 2nd St. / 216-574-9464
www.cleatsgateway.com
The All-American choice. The quintessential sports bar chain's location just behind Quicken Loans Arena is a cozy, intimate stop, so plan to be there by 10 a.m. on game day. Wings are Cleats' claim to fame, but even the finickiest eaters can find something worthwhile on its menu.

Cleveland ChopHouse & Brewery
824 West Saint Clair Ave. / 216-623-0909
www.chophouse.com
Definitely for the leather chair and cigar crowd. This is an elegant, upscale location known for "steak 'n' ale" and a whole host of other classy dishes. Brewmaster Scott Guckel offers a great selection of handcrafted microbrews to warm up late-season Browns games.

The Clevelander Bar & Grill
834 Huron Rd. E. / 216-771-3273
The ultimate "neighborhood bar," with great burgers, old-school video games and more than fifty different bottled beers to choose from. It's not sophisticated, and not supposed to be. Few places feel more truly Cleveland than this.

BARSTOOLGATING

Corner Alley Bar & Grill
402 Euclid Ave. / 216-298-4070
www.thecorneralley.com
Great for the football fans who double as hipsters. It's like a marriage of the movies *Swingers* and *The Big Lebowski*, with a great comfort food menu, sixteen lanes of bowling, martinis and Guinness-battered fish and chips. Strategically placed plasma TVs and a kid-friendly atmosphere make this location great fun.

Fat Fish Blue
21 Prospect Ave. / 216-875-6000
www.fatfishblue.com
Football for the New Orleans enthusiast. If your bag is football, blues music and Creole/ Cajun food, this is your Sunday spot. Get there by 10 a.m. on Sundays or you won't get in, because the jambalaya, crawfish, beignets and pecan pie are a huge draw. It's like a little French Quarter right in the middle of C-Town.

Flat Iron Café
1114 Center St. / 216-696-6968
www.flatironcafe.com
For the fan who likes to "let them do the driving." One of two ideal Irish pub spots, Cleveland's most lauded Irish pub has 100 years of history, an old bar with extravagant woodwork, great imported brews—and a shuttle to and from Browns Stadium. This is a must-stop for Browns fans.

Flannery's Pub
323 West Prospect Ave. / 216-781-7782
www.flannerys.com
Compared to Flat Iron, Flannery's is the new kid on the block. Open since 1997, this Irish pub offers Imperial pints and a spacious dark wood bar. Their tavern features great traditional Irish fare.

Great Lakes Brewing Company

2516 Market Ave. / 216-771-2085
www.greatlakesbrewing.com
Another essential stop for the beer snob or visitor to Cleveland. This award-winning brewery and brewpub features a great beer cellar, twelve regularly available handcrafted beers and savory Cleveland spins on classic dishes. The main taproom once hosted former prohibition agent and Cleveland Director of Public Safety Eliot Ness.

Grille at Gridiron Square

1085 West 3rd St. / 440-824-3436
For the "we'll eat after we get there" crowd. Enclosed at Cleveland Browns Stadium, you need only walk a few feet with your ticket to get inside. Well done American restaurant fare.

Hard Rock Cafe Cleveland

230 Huron Rd. W. / 216-830-7625
www.hardrock.com
With a WKNR 850-AM pregame party featuring on-air personalities Greg Brinda and Aaron Goldhammer, this spot in Tower City Center is lively. You can get there via RTA Rapid Transit and can enjoy breakfast, burgers and beer when you arrive. Convenient for out of town fans staying in the nearby hotels, the Hard Rock's service is quick, the American fare is consistent and the atmosphere is upbeat.

Harry Buffalo

2120 East 4th St. / 216-621-8887
www.harrybuffalo.com
For fans of chain sports bars/restaurants, this sports bar/restaurant located in the Gateway district is familiar almost to a fault. It features namesake Bison Chili, Bullseye Salad and Bison Burgers, and occasionally draws superfans (like "Bubba Dawg" and "Junkyard Dawg") before a big game.

House of Blues

308 Euclid Ave. / 216-523-BLUE

www.hob.com/cleveland

Another great option for visitors to Cleveland. Fans have two options at the live music concert venue during game day: the Gospel Brunch, which features soul food, prime rib, made-to-order omelets and fried chicken; or a stadium-style buffet, fifteen-foot projection TV, $2 Coors drafts and a WTAM 1100 AM Browns pregame show broadcast from the HOB's Cambridge Room. Both start at 10 a.m.

John Q's Steakhouse

55 Public Square / 216-861-0900

www.johnqssteakhouse.com

For those upscale types with mighty appetites. While they don't normally have hours on Sundays during the year, John Q's has an enormous game day brunch that kicks off at 10 a.m.

Johnny's Little Bar & Grill

614 Frankfort Ave. / 216-861-2166

www.johnnyscleveland.com

A true, blue-collar neighborhood bar. The Little Bar is a long-time (and legendary) game day tradition with cliquey customers and satisfyingly cheap eats, and it's also a hangout for bar/restaurant industry workers. They feature a "barbecue/brunch" next door at their anchor location, Johnny's, and there's usually a line to get into either side. The Little Bar is Cleveland's answer to NBC's *Cheers*—everyone there knows everyone else's name.

Liquid Café Fusion

1212 West 6th St. / 216-479-7717

www.liquidliving.com

For the clubbing/nightlife set. From the thumping hip-hop and chart-topping pop tunes to beer for the hard-working Clevelander, this anchor of the entire Warehouse District

always rocks on game day. It's a prime location (and a very short walk from the stadium) and a huge party in a very little space. Get there when it opens. Hours vary.

Local Heroes Grill & Bar

2217 East 9th St. / 216-566-8100
www.localheroesgrill.com
For the all-you-can-eat breakfast fan. This place, across from Jacobs/Progressive Field, opens at 10 a.m. for Browns home games and features a "Sunday Pigskinpalooza" breakfast with bar service for those who still like their kegs and eggs. And they've got a sturdy beer selection.

The Nauti Mermaid

1378 West 6th St. / 216-771-6175
www.thenautimermaid.com
Think coastal, beachside watering hole—Key West meets Maryland. A relatively new Warehouse District staple, this rustic place offers fish tacos, hush puppies and weathered beach bar decor. It's a narrow, intimate spot; Baltimore Ravens fans like it for more than the great draft beer selection.

Panini's Bar & Grille

1290 West 6th St. / 216-523-7070
www.paninisgrill.com

Relive your college experience here. Once a Cleveland Flats staple, Panini's was a post-party location for hungry bar crawlers. Now a local bar/restaurant chain, they still do what they do best: the notorious, Dagwood-like overstuffed sandwich stacked with fries, slaw and thick-cut Italian bread. Great beer list and outdoor patio (during September/ October games).

Pickwick & Frolic Restaurant & Club

2035 East 4th St. / 216-241-7425
www.pickwickandfrolic.com
For the Browns fan who also happens to be a history and entertainment buff. This upscale dining destination houses

the old Cleveland Opera House stage and does have a champagne bar, but it's hardly stuffy. They open at 11 a.m. on Sundays with a huge brunch and HDTVs adorning their beautiful, hardwood bar. Find owner Nick Kostis and he'll tell you all about the history of the place.

Rock Bottom Restaurant & Brewery
2000 Sycamore St., # 260 / 216-623-1555
www.rockbottom.com
For the "get a quick drink and keep moving to the stadium" crowd. Part of a forty-restaurant national chain, this micro-brew pub is better than average and has its share of tasty menu items. Don't expect to linger before a game there. They don't open until 11:30 a.m. on Sundays, so you may want to start early elsewhere.

Sportsman Restaurant
101 St. Clair Ave. / 216-861-5168

For New York expats, transplants and fueling up for those smashmouth Jets and Giants games. This New York-style deli and greasy spoon greets Browns fans with an orange awning and a pair of smiling "fan men" on the outside. In business for over sixty years, the Sportsman wakes at 9 a.m. for fans and offers fantastic corned beef reubens, hot pastrami, breakfast and a full service bar. A Cleveland classic.

The Velvet Dog Niteclub
1280 West 6th St. / 216-664-1116
www.velvetdogcleveland.com
For the Browns fan who will never make the Pro Bowl in Hawaii. One of the more popular stops on a Sunday, the Velvet Dog has a true party atmosphere. During the early part of the season, the tiki lounge-inspired patio plays host to a pregame party/rally with a live rock band, drink specials and a great "in the middle of it all" view of Cleveland's skyline. The party moves to the street as winter encroaches.

Wilbert's

812 Huron Rd. E. / 216-902-4663

www.wilbertsmusic.com

Best location for a Browns/Texans (or Cowboys) game.
This eclectic, roots-music venue is a staple for Indians
and Cavaliers fans due to its proximity. Yet the restaurant's
southwestern flair (quesadillas, spicy beans with dirty rice)
and bar service in the Caxton Building holds wide appeal
to Browns fans as well. Check the Web site for a complete
Sunday schedule before heading over.

Winking Lizard Downtown

811 Huron Rd. E. / 216-589-0313

www.winkinglizard.com

Best location for Browns fans and their kids. The most successful local bar/restaurant chain there is, the downtown
Lizard is packed for nearly every Cleveland sports event.
The hometown sports bar atmosphere, TVs as far as the eye
can see, a solid pub menu and tons of beer options make it
a favorite. Join their two-decades-old Lizard Beer Tour tradition while you're there.

Waterstreet Grill

1265 West 9th St. / 216-619-1600

www.wsgrill.com

For the Browns fan who happens to also be a foodie. This is
a comfy spot for any Browns barstoolgating brunch, given
the Grill's rustic ambiance and splendid comfort food options. The menu features banana walnut pancakes, chicken
paprikash soup (!), grilled salmon with sweet potato fries
and killer mac and cheese. Beer, wine and mimosas are
available all day long.

HOW TO TAILGATE

Preparing for the Tailgate

Once you've scoped out your locations, it's time to formulate a plan. Some Browns tailgaters will tell you that their preparation for a Sunday tailgate starts the moment the previous week's game is completed. If you're that ambitious, that's great, but most people have jobs, families and loads of other personal responsibilities to tend to during off-tailgate hours.

"You've got to have a plan. You just can't wake up and decide to put stuff together that morning. You'll never make it. The people who show up at 8 or 9 a.m. and just start setting up have a lot of work ahead of them without much of a payoff. Getting everything prepared the Friday and Saturday before the game and getting down to your spot early is important. Be prepared for a long day and have a big group of people to help you because it's a lot of work. That's the biggest thing. We try to have different themes, whether it's with food or beverages—basically put a system around which team the

Browns are playing that week. You have to add to it each year. And add new things and new gear to your repertoire to build your tailgate each year." —**Dawg Pound Mike Randall, superfan from Akron**

If you're not mapping out your approach to a Browns tailgate well in advance, you're in for an even longer day than you or your family and friends might anticipate. By and large, the best course of action is to start your prep *no later* than the Friday morning before the game and pick at your checklist throughout the weekend until Sunday morning arrives.

Here are some quick tips to make those shopping trips easy:

- Schedule trips to your favorite market(s), propane tank refilling station and beverage outlet(s) for Thursday or Friday evening, or even Saturday morning if you're really busy during the week. Everything that you need should be purchased by then except for ice—which should be bought right before heading to the lot.

- Check that propane tank before you get to the lot. Watching people run out of gas when the food is only partially done is just sad. All the Browns tailgate locations are without food kiosks and have limited vendors; this bit of planning will keep you from suddenly being faced by an angry mob.

- In order to build an appropriate tailgate shopping list, calculate the number of people you believe will attend your tailgate party, and then add an additional 25 percent to that number. This will come in handy, particularly for food, beverages *and* settings (cups, plates, forks, spoons, knives) and not just for

A fan preps Beer Can Chicken in The Pit just west of Cleveland Browns Stadium. *(Walter Novak)*

the convenience of your own group, but to help in the hospitality toward others in your tailgate location.

- For a typical four-to-six hour tailgate, calculate generously on beverages, both alcoholic and otherwise. There are a number of "drink calculators" available online (on sites like www.eVite.com) that will help you decipher what that magic number for alcohol might be. Consult your favorite beverage store guru for additional help.

- Sunday alcohol sales are starting earlier in some parts of town, but you still don't usually have access to any before 10 a.m. If you wait until then to pick up your adult tailgate beverages, you should probably just take your purchases back home and drink them in front of your TV.

- If you're planning on serving mixed drinks at your tailgate party, you almost have to think like a bartender. Be sure to have at least some of the following mixers on hand: club soda, tonic water, ginger ale, cola (and diet cola), lemon-lime soda. Tomato, orange and cranberry juices are also recommended. All of these mixers cover dozens of mixed drink possibilities.

- Speaking of soft drinks and juices, on average, expect your tailgaters to consume two *non-alcoholic* beverages during the first hour of the party. Then figure on another one each hour from that point on. Make sure you add that to your calculation . . . for that early-season, warm weather game, you'll want to have extra on hand.

- Water: You can *never* have too much. Always plan on carrying two or three personal sized bottles per person. You never know if you'll need it until you don't have it. And that's no time to figure it out.

Outside of the obvious food and drinks—and water, which you'll need for everything from cleanup, to parking lot football injuries to personal hydration—you'll be kicking yourself if you neglect to bring the following things with you:

"Iron Chef" be damned. Some tailgaters just can't do without their kitchen. *(Layne Anderson)*

ESSENTIALS

Tailgate Essentials You'll Wish You'd Remembered

☐ Travel mug of that coffee you made first thing in the morning

☐ Paper towels and napkins

☐ Hand sanitizer and wet naps (wipes, towelettes)

☐ Plastic zipper storage bags and plastic wrap

☐ Tablecloths

☐ As much recyclable material as possible . . . avoid the Styrofoam

☐ Trash bags

☐ Good buns, if you're doing burgers, brats or chicken sandwiches

☐ Bottle opener / can opener/ corkscrew combo

☐ Good, sharp kitchen knife

☐ All necessary cooking supplies

☐ At least two white folding buffet tables

☐ Minimum of two extra-large coolers for food and beverages

☐ Barbecue grill with a full propane tank, or an appropriate amount of charcoal and lighter fluid

☐ Large tent/canopy

☐ Duct tape, rope and something to weight your tent or canopy down on a windy day

☐ Folding chairs (bring some extras for guests)

☐ Toys (at least a Frisbee and football for the kids . . . see others in "Gear")

☐ Beer keg-related equipment (barrel, stand, handle, lines) if you plan to have one

☐ Plastic beverage cups (anything but clear ones . . . we'll explain that later)

☐ Several large bags of ice from the local gas station or convenience store for your coolers

☐ Jerseys, flags, banners and various other Browns-related flair

☐ . . . and don't forget your *tickets* if you're going to the game!

Really, Just One More Thing About Water

Seriously, I know I'm overdoing it here, but whatever you do, *don't* forget to bring water with you. It's not readily available at any of the Browns tailgate locations and, based on what I've seen, you'll need it for *everything*. I've seen people pass out in the parking lots from the heat (and other assorted reasons) during pre-season and into September. For everything from extinguishing your bonfire and charcoal grill to any potential emergency that could arise, it's absolutely *essential*.

Here Comes Sunday Morning

The earlier you can start on Sunday morning, the better your chances of having a great experience. **Allow yourself a cushion of up to two hours** to set up your tailgate camp and don't let your set-up time infringe on your party time if you can help it. The best way to avoid that snag is to bring as many of your tailgate party pals down with you to the lot to help set everything up.

What Time to Show Up?

Unless you're unable to commit to such an early schedule, plan to be in your designated space *no later than* 7 a.m. This way, with that two-hour set up time, you'll be whipping up your breakfast or brunch by 9 a.m. And if you have a lot of help, your party will start even earlier than that.

Ah Yes, But Where to Show Up?

This is *critical*. Choosing a parking lot and a space to tailgate is as important as any of the prep work done beforehand. Find a location (see previous chapter) that feels the most comfortable for you and your group; don't be afraid to experiment with a few different locations until you find the right fit. Aim for a spot with a view of Cleveland Browns Stadium if you can, and try to find a good spot that allows for maximum social interaction with other tailgaters.

Start off on the right foot and bear your tailgate neighbors in mind . . . because the odds are, *they've been at it longer than you.* Consideration for those Browns fans who arrived in the lot before you will go a long way toward making your game day experience a better one. When you're getting ready to pull in to a particular space, you may receive some direction (in either a kind or unfriendly manner) from others already camped near there.

If your neighbors tell you that a particular space near them is reserved for someone else, don't be rude about it in return or park there anyway. If you do, you can expect the same thing you would in your own neighborhood—a cold shoulder at best. Instead, ask for some advice on what other spaces around them are available. They'll appreciate it and might even offer you a bite or a drink once you're settled. They might end up being your tailgating buds.

The Party

Once your camp is all set up, start cooking, put on the tunes and break out the beverages. Put a couple of people in charge of food preparation and keeping everything on the grill and the buffet tables rotated. Make sure that all of the necessary food, drinks and accoutrements are appropriately labeled with Post-It notes, so your partiers know what they're scooping onto their plates.

Clean Up and Tear Down

Run your list that helped you pack for your tailgate in reverse and plan to spend some time packing everything away. Be sure to clean up after yourself and use the old

Tailgating is not limited to football. Fans of NASCAR and Indy auto racing, basketball, baseball, hockey, soccer, touring musical acts and (most recently) kids' sporting events tailgate regularly before their favorite events. Keep an eye out at that next big event. You're liable to see more than a few diehard tailgaters when you get there.

camping/hiking adage, "leave no trace." Throw away your trash in available trashcans or bags that you've brought along, and safely dispose of any hot coals from your grill. Leave as little as possible for the giant garbage sweepers run by the City of Cleveland (which are like those colossal leaf collection trucks you see in the fall). Hang around late enough after a game, and you're likely to see one.

One More Thing

Themes for a tailgate can be really cool. Spend enough time in the Browns tailgate parking lots around the holidays and you'll see Halloween, Thanksgiving and Christmas celebrated before your very eyes. When AFC North teams are in town, look for themes mocking the opposition. Some people even use food as a theme (regional favorites from the opposing team . . . use your imagination!).

Away Games in the AFC North

Think you've got what it takes to hit the road and tailgate for a Browns away game? If you think the planning for tailgating at home is a challenging proposition, but you're up to it (or have already mastered it), then your next step is to hit the road and follow the team to the competing AFC North rival locations: Baltimore, Cincinnati and Pittsburgh.

> "Away games are always a great time to be had, but they require some serious planning ahead. We plot out our road trips, airfare, hotel accommodations

and align ourselves with quality people out of town well in advance—usually right after the schedule for the season is announced. We have allegiance with NFL 'superfans' across the country. We take care of them when they come to Cleveland and they take care of us. That's key to making sure you have a successful trip—that and traveling to those games with people you're comfortable with."
—*Dawg Pound Mike Randall*

Pull your travel plans together with some help from the Internet and the American Automobile Association (a.k.a. Triple-A, AAA) or, if you plan to meet friends out of town and tailgate with them, consult your local travel agent and favorite mapping and travel Web sites. These recommendations will help you formulate your road trip game plan:

BALTIMORE

The Baltimore Ravens play at M&T Bank Stadium, located at 1101 Russell St., Baltimore, MD, 21230. The stadium, which opened in 1998, has a capacity of 70,008 and sits in the city center's Harbor District. Getting to the stadium is easy with the Maryland Transit Administration (MTA), which operates bus, rail and subway service to M&T Bank stadium.

Stadium tours: Must be planned in advance, and only for groups of twenty-five or more—so be sure to connect with other tailgaters if you're angling to do this. Once you've got your interested parties together, call 410-261-7283.

Tailgate parking hints: All Maryland Stadium Authority lots allow tailgating; the most raucous is "Lot J," where you'll find the vast majority of the RVs. The "Ravens Walk" is also pretty festive. It's located between M&T Bank Stadium and Oriole

Park at Camden Yards, sandwiched between parking lots B and C. Most of the parking lots open five hours before kickoff (Lot J opens at 7 a.m. for a 1 p.m. kickoff). Parking there ranges from $20 to 25, with prices varying elsewhere.

Stay overnight: Pier 5 Hotel (711 Eastern Ave., 410-539-2000) is a comfortably hip waterfront hotel. It's about a mile away from M&T Bank Stadium, but it is right in the middle of downtown Baltimore's action, features a Ruth's Chris steakhouse inside and is a short walk from the Power Plant entertainment complex.

Baltimore Flavors: This seafaring metropolis is a hub for great seafood, so don't miss out. You can get everything from traditional padded oyster stew and seafood chowder to buttery crab in town. Recommendations include:

★ Clipper City Brewing Co. beer (varieties): *www.ccbeer.com*

★ Faidley's Blue Crab lump crabcakes: *www.faidleyscrabcakes.com*

★ Maryland Panfried Chicken at The New Duffy's: *www.newduffysrestaurant.com*

★ Attman's Pastrami and other deli flavors: *www.attmansdeli.com*

★ Schultz's Raw Bar: *www.schultzs.com*

★ And if you're really daring, try to get a bite of "Lady Raven 127's Crab Dip" in Lot J of M&T Bank Stadium. It's delightful . . . *if* you can get any while dressed as a Browns fan.

Baltimore Barstoolgating: If you weren't able to procure a ticket while tailgating, most locals will point you in the direction of Pratt Street, the Inner Harbor, or Federal Hill for your game time partying/viewing. Lots of great watering holes in all three locations; the Inner Harbor takes it up a notch with fresh sushi, seafood, billiards and the original "ESPN Zone" sports bar and arcade. Learn about all three party boroughs by visiting www.baltimore.org. The Cat's Eye Pub (1730 Thames St., 410-276-9866) in the Fell's Point shipyard district is also popular as a live music-and-food spot.

Attractions & Sightseeing: The districts mentioned in "Barstoolgating" are also huge draws for out-of-town visitors. Make a plan to hit at least one of them on the way to the National Aquarium of Baltimore (501 East Pratt St., 410-576-3800). It's a must-see that packs 'em in during the summer months. When you're done, walk down the street to learn about the history of the city and take in its best views at the Top of the World Observation Level and Museum at Baltimore's World Trade Center (401 East Pratt St., 410-837-8439).

Trivia: Baltimore has the only NFL team that features a marching band during its games. This dates back to the Baltimore (now Indianapolis) Colts and that team's marching band that used to perform at Memorial Stadium. The Johnny Unitas Memorial Plaza at M&T Bank Stadium—named for the Colts' legendary quarterback—offers another nod to the city's football past. Former Browns owner Art Modell reportedly considered tailgate-friendly rules a priority for Ravens fans when he moved the original Browns team east; shortly after the team arrived, Baltimore passed laws to help make Sunday tailgating a better experience.

CINCINNATI

The Cincinnati Bengals play at Paul Brown Stadium, located at One Paul Brown Stadium, Cincinnati, OH 45202. The stadium, which opened in 2000, has a capacity of 65,535 and is located in downtown Cincinnati. The city's Metro transit system allows for easy access to the stadium.

Stadium tours: Stadium tours (during the summer only) can be arranged by calling 513-455-4805.

Tailgate parking hints: Tailgating is permitted in most lots around the stadium; the best for tailgating are the CG&E parking lot on Mehring Way at the riverfront and along Second St. west of the stadium. Lots are open by 7 a.m. Parking ranges from $15 to 30.

Stay overnight: The Westin Cincinnati Hotel (21 East 5th St., 513-621-7700) is not just classy, but it's only a short walk from Paul Brown Stadium and overlooks the city's historic Fountain Square. The hotel is within walking distance from a fair number of other attractions, for Browns fans who are looking to make an entire weekend of it.

Cincinnati Flavors: The Queen City has some really distinctive food options because of where they're positioned on the map. With Kentucky (and even nearby West Virginia) as influences, the gastronomic options are very worthwhile. Suggestions include:

★   Christian Moerlein beer (varieties): *www.christianmoerlein.com*

★   Skyline Chili & Goldstar Chili (a three-way): *www. skylinechili.com; www.goldstarchili.com*

★ Izzy's Corned Beef and Potato Pancakes: *www.izzys.com*

★ Montgomery Inn Ribs and Barbecue: *www.montgomeryinn.com*

★ A fried bologna sandwich (a Midwestern treat that skipped Cleveland somehow).

★ Glier's Goetta: www.goetta.com (technically a German breakfast sausage from Covington, Kentucky, but very popular in Cincinnati. It is made up of pork, beef, "pinhead oats," and seasonings. Slice up this dense meat delicacy and panfry or grill for a flavor recalling Philadelphia "scrapple.")

Cincinnati Barstoolgating: Ask ten different Cincinnati Bengals fans where the best place is to take in the game and you'll get ten different answers. "Who Dey?" indeed. For our money, the Crooked Nail Tavern (9303 Cincinnati-Columbus Rd., 513-755-7800) with a great beer selection and the best fish fry in the Queen City is the choice. In Between Tavern (307 Sycamore St., 513-621-1000) is similarly stocked, warm and friendly—even when faced with opposition fans. And if you want to have a really gritty sports bar experience, Rockin' Robin's Rock 'N Sports Bar (10 West 7th St., 513-621-1000) is tops.

Attractions & Sightseeing: While Carew Tower (441 Vine St., 513-241-3888) in downtown Cincinnati offers the best view of the city from up high, BB Riverboat Cruises offer the best views of the riverfront, great food and a number of different cruise options on three different sternwheelers—the *Mark Twain, River Queen* and *Cincinnati Belle* (101 Riverboat Row, Newport, KY, 800-261-8586).

Trivia: Paul Brown Stadium is named for the legendary Paul Brown of Cleveland Browns fame. Brown was the father of modern football, notoriously fired by former Browns owner, Art Modell. Paul Brown Stadium was the backdrop for now retired Bengals running back Corey Dillon, who rushed for a record 278 yards in one game against the Denver Broncos. That record has since been broken, but that doesn't stop Bengals fans from talking it up.

PITTSBURGH

The Pittsburgh Steelers play at Heinz Field, located at 400 Art Rooney Ave., Pittsburgh, PA 15212. The stadium, which opened in 2001, has a capacity of 65,050 and is located a little over one mile northwest of the center of town. The Port of Allegheny County operates bus service to Heinz Field.

Stadium tours: Available from time to time. Call 412-697-7150 for details.

Tailgate parking hints: RVs and other larger vehicles should park on the side of the stadium next to the Carnegie Science Center, which is directly across the street from the field. The Gold Lots are the liveliest, but there is tailgating in the North Side lots as well. Parking ranges from $15 to 30.

Stay overnight: There are two great options. First, the Renaissance Pittsburgh Hotel (107 6th St., 412-562-1200) is in close range of Heinz Field, PNC Park (where Major League Baseball's Pirates play) and Mellon Arena (where the National Hockey League's Penguins play). Operated by Marriott, it's located in the restored Fulton Building with a quaint, comfortable environment that could be a treat for the spouse who might be getting dragged along. Much in the same vein, the Hilton Pittsburgh (600 Commonwealth Place,

412-391-4600) has undergone an extensive renovation and is a lavish destination re-opened just in time for the 2008 NFL season.

Pittsburgh Flavors: As you might expect, there is a great deal of "culinary crossover" between rival cities Pittsburgh and Cleveland—barbecue chipped ham, pierogies, bratwurst, sauerkraut, kielbasa and more. Pittsburgh even has Primanti Bros. (www.primantibrothers.com), a restaurant that offers a "Dagwood"-style sandwich—much like Cleveland's Panini's sandwich, with fries and slaw *on the sandwich.* But there's one thing in Pittsburgh that you absolutely can't get in Cleveland and according to the brewers, you won't find here anytime soon: Yuengling beer.

Yuengling is "America's Oldest Brewery" and they're located in Pottsville, Pennsylvania. Their traditional, light amber lager is one of the tastiest beverages to be had in the entire AFC North. They distribute to ten different states and the District of Columbia, but not Ohio. (It figures, you can get it in *Baltimore*, too!) Yuengling's Lager is flavorful enough to appeal to the microbrewery crowd, yet light enough that mainstream beer fans will enjoy it, too. And they have several other varieties (including a tasty Black & Tan) to add to their appeal. The lack of availability in Ohio has made Yuengling a cult favorite among local beer drinkers; even though you're not supposed to transport beer across state lines, a lot of Browns fans make a regular habit of bringing Yuengling back with them, uh, as a *souvenir.* Yeah, that's it.

Yuengling beats the stuffing out of Iron City Beer, that pale lager beer that used to feature Steelers Super Bowl teams on their labels back in the day. Browns fans will tell you IC is thin, flavorless and has a consistency of beer-flavored sparkling water. Or *worse* . . . all depends on who you ask.

Pittsburgh Barstoolgating: Browns fans looking for a good vibe should check out Finnigan's Wake (20 East General Robinson St., 412-325-2601, www.finniganspittsburgh.com) and McFadden's (211 North Shore Dr., 412-322-3470, www.mcfaddenspitt.com). These Irish-themed sports bars are high-energy and generally pretty accepting of out-of-town fans (yes, *even* Clevelanders!) If you're looking for something a touch more sophisticated, former Steelers running back Jerome Bettis' Grille 36 (393 North Shore Dr., 412-224-6287, www.jeromebettisgrille36.com) is a posh spot. With a swanky wine list and more than fifty (count 'em) HDTVs scattered throughout, it's a crowd-pleaser.

A Tip on Spirits: Whatever you do, don't forget to buy your carry-out beer and liquor for your tailgate in Pittsburgh on a Saturday. Liquor sales are prohibited on Sundays in Pennsylvania—so if you don't bring it with you or plan ahead, your tailgate will be a dry one. What's more, keep in mind that liquor is sold only at state-run stores . . . so if you need a "handle" (bottle of liquor) *and* beer for your 'gate, be prepared to make two stops to get them.

Attractions & Sightseeing: The way the schedule has gone since 1999, if you're headed to Pittsburgh, you should expect a cold, late season game. A lot of hipsters swear by the Warhol Museum (117 Sandusky St., 412-237-8300) and it's hard to disagree. And no trip to Pittsburgh would be complete without a trip down the Duquesne Incline (1220 Grandview Ave., 412-381-1665), a working museum that has been taking passengers down a funicular (hillside) railway, with great views of the Golden Triangle of Pittsburgh, since 1877.

Trivia: Heinz Field has two large and prominently-placed Heinz ketchup bottles that sit on top of their JumboTron scoreboard. When the Steelers reach the Red Zone (inside their opponent's 20-yard line) these imitation condiments "pour" ketchup all over the scoreboard. Also related to condiments, locals call Heinz Field "the Mustard Palace" due to its yellow seats.

Away Games Outside the AFC North

If you're looking to tailgate for games outside the AFC North, don't be the least bit surprised at the number of Browns fans who are headed in the same direction you're planning to head in. Walking through Detroit Metro Airport at 4:30 a.m. on a Monday, you wouldn't expect to see a group of bleary-eyed Browns fans on a red-eye flight layover when the team was just playing in Phoenix. *But you will.* Do yourself a favor: get networked in to all of the Browns fans online and you might find yourself in the midst of those sleepy, jersey-clad fans in an airport.

> "What's really amazing to me is seeing all of these Browns tailgaters on the road. Not just the transplants that live elsewhere, but the same people from here at all the away games! Average Browns fans just don't see that, or know that they do this sort of thing. There are all these people out on the road. In Arizona last season, we're out there at the new University of Arizona Stadium for the Browns/Cardinals game, and in the hotels and parking lots near the stadium, they're everywhere.

"I remember [Browns receiver/special teams player] Josh Cribbs sitting on the team bus right next to me, and we're driving by these places in Glendale on the way to the stadium and he's like, 'Damn!' There were Browns fans jam-packed in the parking lot of a mini-mall in Glendale, Arizona, and we're both like 'Man, they've brought Cleveland to Glendale!' It just gives you chills. You're left with this 'I can't believe this' feeling, man. It was awesome."
—Andre Knott, WTAM 1100 Browns beat reporter

If you're planning on heading outside the AFC North to tailgate, or you're looking for a group to tailgate with, then your best bet is to start scoping things out ahead of time online. You can follow who is traveling where in the Browns tailgating realm by watching the many **Browns fan sites on MySpace.com**. A quick Google search will help you find them. There are also **a number of great Web sites** out there that have collected information on each NFL city—all with the idea of helping travelers from across the globe to get to their football destination:

Joe "The Commissioner" Cahn's Tailgating Site: **www.tailgate.com**

Johnny Road Trip: **www.johnnyroadtrip.com**

The American Tailgater's Association: **www.atatailgate.com**

United States Tailgating Association: **www.ustga.com**

Cleveland Browns Backers Worldwide

And of course, the Cleveland Browns Backers could be your biggest resource of all. With 300-plus chapters and nearly 87,000 members all across the globe, the Backers groups represent the ultimate social networking situation for Cleveland Browns fans in Cleveland and beyond. The Backers are one of the largest and most organized fan clubs in all of professional sport.

When you join the Browns Backers Worldwide, you gain access to hundreds of Browns fans in your immediate vicinity and tons of Browns fans and Cleveland expatriates in other NFL cities. Visit www.clevelandbrowns.com/fans/backers to learn more about the Backers and the group nearest you.

Then the next time the team travels to expat strongholds for former Clevelanders like Phoenix (the largest Browns Backers organization outside of Ohio is the Southwest Browns Backers there, with 2,069 members) Miami or San Diego (often referred to as "Dawg Pound West" by fans) you're covered.

One of the most constant and legendary tailgate parties isn't connected to a sporting event at all. The Grateful Dead—considered the longest touring band in popular music history—took tailgating to the nth degree during their heyday. Their counterculture fan base of "Deadheads" followed them across the country, setting up pre-show camps and supporting their never-ending tailgate lifestyle by selling tie-dyed shirts, incense, homemade jewelry, burritos, snacks and other goods.

The Gear

It doesn't take much poking around on the Internet to figure out who is promoting what kind of tailgate equipment. Joe "The Commissioner" Cahn, for example, has a whole page on his Web site devoted to "Tailgating Gear" at www.tailgating.com. And he's not the only one. However, the best advice on what variety of gear to use comes from the fans themselves.

If you're considering a tailgating pilgrimage in the near future, make an effort to talk to tailgaters and ask them what gear they recommend. More often than not, Browns tailgaters with an elaborate set-up have a great deal of experience "field testing" everything from the right grill and cooler to the right tent, canopy and winter coat with Thinsulate lining.

The Essentials . . . Start with Research

Before you've been though that "List of Tailgate Essentials You'll Wish You'd Remembered" in an earlier chapter, it helps to have done your research about gas grills, comfortable seating, tables, tents/canopies, generators and other no-brainers. There are plenty of recommendations to be made, but it really all comes down to what level of comfort you are used to, or may feel stranded without.

Take a Sunday and go down to a Browns tailgate location and talk to some people.

In his survey, Joe Cahn determined that most tailgaters weren't of the "fair-weather" variety. Literally. Some 84 percent of tailgaters he surveyed said that weather conditions had no bearing on their tailgating habits. "And, tailgaters don't avoid the parking lot even if their home team isn't winning on the gridiron," Cahn says. "There really aren't any 'rebuilding years' when it comes to tailgating."

Take notes, see what people are using and ask plenty of questions. Then head home, log on to your computer and check out Web sites like www.eopinions.com, www.amazon.com and others. These are great places to get a feel for any and every kind of gear that is available to the tailgating fan.

Thinking about buying a Camp Kitchen by Coleman or a rechargeable blender? Maybe you're thinking sleeping bags for that Muni Lot campout on Saturday night? Or perhaps the thought crossed your mind that, rather than freezing to death in the Burke Lot or in The Pit, you should have an appropriate twenty-below parka with goose down stuffing . . . ?

Protecting Yourself Against the Elements

"Dress appropriately." If your mom is like mine, you've heard it ever since you were old enough to tie your shoes. But it stands as a word of warning, especially for spectators and tailgaters. Comfort is key and no one likes being unprepared when facing the elements. It can make agony of an otherwise enjoyable time.

Fans from more mild climates and domed stadium teams don't have to deal with the exceptional temperature swings during the NFL season like Midwestern/ heartland teams do. Think Green Bay, Buffalo, Chicago and yes, even Pittsburgh. *We* all have to deal with a wide variety of changeable weather. It can snow in September and it can be seventy degrees in late December.

With that in mind, having plenty of personal temperature and weather options on hand is a good thing:

ESSENTIALS

☐ During the preseason, **t-shirts, shorts, flip-flops and sunscreen** are essential, with tennis shoes, socks and a rain slicker/poncho as a good call for back-up. And don't forget your cap. No one likes late summer sunburn.

☐ September and October are always unpredictable, particularly in Cleveland. The wind whipping off Lake Erie can change a perfectly beautiful day into a downright chilly proposition . . . unless you've been imbibing and can't feel it. Best advice? **Layers, layers, layers** . . . and make sure at least one is water-resistant or waterproof. You never know when it might rain, and you can always add or remove layers.

☐ In November, December and into the NFL Playoffs (I know, dare to dream . . . but we're going this time!) **prepare for Antarctica.** Carhartt, Thinsulate, Eddie Bauer, L.L. Bean, Lands' End . . . whatever outdoor outfitter's gear it takes to get you warm and keep you warm, make sure you've got it. And think headgear, scarves, gloves, mittens, hand and foot warmers, blankets and other bundling materials while you're at it. You can never have too much.

☐ Finally (yes, we're going there again) consider hydration as much of a must-have emergency item as the cell phone in your pocket and the jumper cables in your trunk. You do have both of those, right?

Fans take in the pre-game show in the DumDawg Bus, which features satellite TV and is wired for sound. *(Layne Anderson)*

Big Generator

Really want to "up the ante" of luxury and excess for your tailgate? With all the electrical and electronic gear you might wish to set up in one of the famed Browns tailgate locations, finding the right **portable generator or marine battery** to run it all is the key. You'll want to pick out something relatively light, weight-wise (100 pounds or less), and as compact as possible to avoid taking up unnecessary space in your vehicle. Shoot for a generator with four-gallon fuel capacity and around 4,000 watts of power.

You'll get anywhere between five to eight hours of run time, depending on what gear you're planning to use. And best of all, if you need to run heating units or other critical emergency gear with it, you'll have the power to do so. As with other items mentioned earlier, do your research and consult an expert before "powering up".

And Now, for Something Completely Eccentric . . .

While I can't exactly recommend these items for purchase (didn't see any of them in action or try them in person, and not sure I'd want to) they all looked interesting enough to merit a quick mention. If you're looking to start a conversation (or, in the case of one of these items, end one) consider these three tailgating items:

- **The "Trailer Hitch Hammock".** This unit accommodates two suspended chairs from the trailer hitch of most pickup trucks and other active-use vehicles. It looks like fun, and perhaps is better for the beach, but sadly not very practical. It looks cool, though. Will definitely get you some looks. www.hammaka.com.

- **The "Beerbelly" and "Winerack".** These are hands-free gadgets that are worn as undergarments and resemble a spare tire and breast augmentation, respectively. Yup, use that imagination of yours. Fanatical tailgaters might consider wearing one of these odd devices, which hold a significant amount of your favorite beverage. The company that sells these will have you believe that people walk into the game wearing them, too. We'll leave you to figure that one out. www.thebeerbelly.com.

- **The "Stadium Pal".** With bathrooms at a minimum for tailgating at Browns games, you might wonder how you're going to handle nature's call. You could make friends with a tailgater who has a super-deluxe vehicle with a bathroom, wait for one of the few porta-potties in the Muni Lot, or experience nature's call, well, *in nature*. The Stadium Pal is one other possible solution. With an external catheter coupling that resembles a condom, this gadget can be worn during a tailgate or a game, thereby avoiding the need for a restroom altogether. And yes, there's also a Stadium *Gal*. As eccentric as it gets . . . is it getting warm in here, *or is it just me?* www. stadiumpal.com.

Sporting Your Fandom

It's one thing to pick out your favorite player's jersey from a sporting goods store or local big box retail outlet. But it's another thing altogether to have something customized and truly original—whether it is a special order from www.nfl. com or something that you concocted in your basement or garage.

Left: With one X-Acto knife and five patient minutes, your old Tim Couch jersey becomes an ironic conversation piece.

Below: Laura Hlebak's old Kelly Holcomb jersey becomes a new Brady Quinn jersey with a little old fashioned ingenuity. *(Peter Chakerian)*

Perhaps you have a nickname at your tailgate like "Fritz," or a specific location you always party at The Pit or the Muni Lot, or maybe you have a dislike for a former player like Tim Couch. Having a customized shirt, jersey, or other piece of team apparel has always been a way to show devotion to your Browns.

But don't think that you have to spend money in pursuit of a cool, wearable fan conversation piece. Be creative! As the photos here show, an X-Acto knife can turn that old Tim Couch jersey from the bottom of your closet into a totally appropriate "Ouch" jersey. And those old Kelly Holcomb jerseys? Well, they're just a swatch of wide electrical/duct tape and a permanent marker away from being a "brand new" (natch) Brady Quinn jersey.

(Matt Edwards)

A Great and Functional Non-Costume Costume Option

The "Backerbib." If you're thinking you might like to dress up, but you're just not that radical, and you're looking for something functional because you'll be cooking all day. These overalls are durable and feature a one-inch vertical stripe pattern in Browns colors. They're pretty cool (as this picture suggests). www.backerbibs.com.

Last Minute Apparel Shopping and "Bootlegs"

Didn't have time to pick something out from the closet, the store or the Internet before you headed down for Sunday tailgating? Keep an eye out for the myriad vendors who are stationed along East 9th Street, North and South Marginal Roads and wandering the lots with shopping carts full of interesting Browns and other sports-related gear. The quality of some of these items can be called into question, so as the old saying goes, "buyer beware."

Two things are certain: 1) if you forgot that wool hat, headband for your ears or other essential bit of personal gear or apparel, you're likely to find it by wandering around a little on Sunday morning . . . if the vendors don't find you first. 2) There's no way you'll find some of the apparel (including the one pictured here) at Target or Wal-Mart.

Tailgating Games

There's more going on in the parking lots than just throwing the football or Frisbee around these days. If you're looking to add some gamesmanship and competitive spirit to your

(Peter Chakerian)

Waiting their turn: A "TailgateDawg" and friends play a spirited round of "Beanbags"—a.k.a. "Cornhole."
(Peter Chakerian)

Browns tailgate experience, check out some of the tailgating games you can partake in while you're hanging with your crew in the parking lot. You'll see all of these games (and other made-up events and pseudo-carnival events) happening all over the parking lots. Simply pop one of these games into your favorite Internet search engine and you'll get an idea of how to play, where to find/buy the game, or plans on how to build one of your own. They're also great options for home tailgating, which we'll briefly cover a little bit later:

- 🏈 **Football Toss (a.k.a. Spiral Toss).** Exactly as described. If you can get past the cheesy Levitra jokes, it can be a lot of fun. Watch the action in the Muni Lot, right near the southeast entrance to the North Coast lot.

- 🏈 **Cornhole (a.k.a. Beanbags, Corn Toss, Bag-o, Tailgate Toss, 21).** Like a cross between the old 1970s game "Toss-Across" and horseshoes. The game boards are placed anywhere between twenty and twenty-five feet apart. Each team of two players alternates throws of their four large beanbags, aiming for the board. Get a beanbag on the board and score a point; get one in the hole and you score three points. Score twenty-one points and your team wins. People actually build their own boards now.

- 🏈 **Washer Pitching (a.k.a. Texas Toss).** Played on a smaller board than Cornhole, two similar teams take turns tossing quarter-sized steel plumbing washers onto a board with a hole and painted target. There are some variations out there now that resemble Cornhole boards, except that they're longer and have more holes. Scoring varies on where the washer lands; most people play to a score of twenty-one.

Turning ping-pong on its ear: a friendly game of Beer Pong livens up this Muni Lot tailgate. *(Layne Anderson)*

- **Ladder Golf (a.k.a. Hillbilly Golf, Bolo Toss, Ladder Ball, Gate Golf).** Teams are configured the same as for Cornhole. Each team has a number of "Bolos" (two golfballs attached with nylon rope) and must throw them toward the opposing "Ladder." Scoring varies with which rung the bolo lands on, with scoring to (you guessed it) twenty-one.

- **The Giant Tower (a.k.a. Lifesized Jenga).** With wooden pieces cut from wooden two-by-fours, two players or teams take turns removing a piece of the block tower and placing it strategically on the top of the remaining pieces. Game continues until the tower comes down; if you bring the tower down, you lose. A lot of people are building these set-ups; you can cut four pieces out of a two-by-four eight-foot wooden plank. More fun than a dizzy bat race!

- **Beer Pong (a.k.a. Beirut, Lob Cup, Lob Pong).** Two players (or a pair of two-player teams) stand opposite of each other at a long, narrow table (usually buffet-sized). Each player lobs a ping pong ball toward a triangle configuration of ten beer-filled plastic cups pointed toward them. The object is to land a ball in the opponent's cups of beer, which must then be consumed by the defending team. Eliminate all of the other team's cups and you win.

🏈 **Flipcup (a.k.a. Boat Race).** This is a simple two-person drinking race, where contestants stand across from each other at a table. A race to consume the same amount of beer (or other beverage) in a cup is followed by leaving the cup hanging just over the edge of the table. Contestants then have to turn the cup over on the table by flipping it; they must repeat this step over and over until one person's cup stands upside down on the table. Sometimes multiple cups are used in a race.

🏈 **Parking Lot Quarters (a.k.a. Giant Quarters).** Just like the popular drinking game, where players bounce a quarter off of a bar or table and into a shot glass . . . except that the bouncing of the quarter sometimes happens off the pavement in the parking lot. Land your quarter in the cup (or an old coffee can) and your opponent must consume a tasty beverage.

(Layne Anderson)

🏈 **Beer Bong Races.** A favorite among fraternities and sororities on college campuses across the country. Two people race to consume a beverage, with the help of gravity, out of a funnel-and-tube apparatus. The person who finishes their beverage first wins. The Braylon Bunch takes this game to a whole new level.

Dawg Pound Mike Randall's camp—complete with custom vehicle, old style speakers and inflatable linebacker. *(Layne Anderson)*

Sounds From the Pound

Choosing the perfect playlist for a tailgate party doesn't *sound* like a big deal, but if you've read this far you know that everything about Browns tailgating is a big deal. Finding the right music to fit the mood of the tailgate party is important and can be much more complicated than just hitting amazon.com, the local Best Buy for ESPN's *Jock Jams* or downloading the whole "Game Day Party" playlist on iTunes.

That quick-fix approach works in a pinch, but each and every person has a different idea of what playlist is going to pump up their group and rock their party to maximum effect before the big game. Music sets the tone for the en-

Jimmy Buffett fans, or "Parrot-heads" as they're known, regularly claim to be the most rabid non-sports related tailgaters in the United States. On the hundreds of Buffett fan Web sites online, you'll find these fans coordinating each and every detail of each tailgate surrounding a summer Buffett tour. The jury's still out on if a "Cheeseburger in Paradise" is the most consumed food item at a Parrothead tailgate party.

ESSENTIAL ROCK/ HEAVY METAL TRACKS

GUNS N' ROSES "Welcome to the Jungle," "You Could Be Mine"

METALLICA "Enter Sandman," "For Whom the Bell Tolls"

AC/DC "Thunderstruck," "Back in Black," "Highway to Hell," "Hell's Bells," "A Long Way to the Top," "TNT"

ROLLING STONES "Start Me Up," "You Can't Always Get What You Want"

VELVET REVOLVER "Slither"

KISS "Rock and Roll All Nite"

JUDAS PRIEST "You've Got Another Thing Coming"

PANTERA "Walk," "Far Beyond Driven"

QUEEN "We Will Rock You/We Are the Champions," "Stone Cold Crazy"

VAN HALEN "Unchained," "Right Now"

GEORGE THOROGOOD & THE DESTROYERS "Bad to the Bone," "Move it on Over"

BLACK SABBATH "War Pigs," "Paranoid"

WHITESNAKE "Still of the Night"

MOTLEY CRUE "Kickstart My Heart," "Wildside," "Girls, Girls, Girls"

OZZY OSBOURNE "Crazy Train," "I Don't Wanna Stop"

STEPPENWOLF "Born to be Wild"

THE WHO "Won't Get Fooled Again," "Baba O'Reilly"

ESSENTIAL COUNTRY TAILGATE TRACKS

GARTH BROOKS "Friends in Low Places," "Two Piña Coladas," "Rodeo"

TOBY KEITH "I Love This Bar," "Beer for My Horses" (with Willie Nelson)

TIM MCGRAW "I Like It, I Love It"

BRAD PAISLEY "Alcohol"

GRETCHEN WILSON "Here for the Party," "Redneck Woman"

tire tailgate, and if you've been to a tailgate party, you know that there are plenty of sounds coming from all across the parking lot— many amateur DJs and variety of tunes competing for the humble tailgater's ears.

Picking Your Playlist

Like most of us, the odds are you don't have the cash lying around to hire a rock band or a professional DJ to play your individual tailgate. So what's a Browns tailgater to do? How should one go

KID ROCK "Cowboy," "All Summer Long"

KENNY CHESNEY "Keg in the Closet," "No Shirt, No Shoes, No Problems"

MARTINA MCBRIDE "This One's for the Girls"

ALAN JACKSON "Don't Rock the Jukebox"

BON JOVI "I Love This Town"

JIMMY BUFFETT "Margaritaville"

GEORGE STRAIT w/HANK THOMPSON "Six Pack to Go"

REBECCA LYNN HOWARD "I Need a Vacation"

HANK WILLIAMS, JR. "All My Rowdy Friends"

CRAIG MORGAN "Redneck Yacht Club"

THE CHARLIE DANIELS BAND "Devil Went Down to Georgia"

JIMMY BUFFETT & ALAN JACKSON "It's Five O'Clock Somewhere"

TRACE ADKINS "(This Ain't) No Thinkin' Thing"

ROBERT EARL KEEN "Barbeque"

JASON & THE SCORCHERS "One More Day of Weekend"

THE GREAT DIVIDE "Pour Me a Vacation"

RASCAL FLATTS "Life is a Highway"

about picking their individual DJ playlist for game day? It's all a matter of personal taste, knowing your audience and not *cheesing out* (that is, playing too much chart-topping teeny-bopper music). A successful DJ in a tailgate lot should aim for the following:

- maintaining a level of energy and enthusiasm to keep your group fired up;

- smooth transitions between songs;

- keeping the beat between mid-tempo songs (say Nickelback's "Rockstar") and up-tempo songs (like AC/DC's "Thunderstruck");

- aim for a good mix of sing-along songs and adrenaline pumpers that people might actually hear later at the stadium during the game;

- keep the ladies dancing and the guys' heads bobbing.

It's a tall order, to be sure. And in the end, rocking your tunes at a tailgate party is also an individual call and subject to personal taste. There many different ways to go about it finding that right mix. Amateurs can hunt up ESPN's many *Jock Jams* and *Stadium Anthems* CDs; pick up other locally-focused CDs like *Cleveland Rocks: Music from The Drew Carey Show* and *Cleveland Browns Greatest Hits: Songs & Live Calls that Rock the Dawg Pound* and start your mix there; you can spend a day or two polling friends for what they would like to hear; you could do a little digging online to find out which "bumper music" that your favorite sports talk radio show hosts play before and after commercials.

Or, you could spend a few games trolling all of the Cleveland tailgate spots and perking up your ears for many of these recommended songs, as heard in all of the Browns tailgate lots on Sunday mornings:

Tailgating Audio Gear

For tailgaters who haven't crossed over into the built-in sound systems in custom vehicle territory (see "Tailgate Rides"), there are still many options to keep the tunes rocking in the parking lot.

ESSENTIAL MODERN/ALT-ROCK TRACKS

RAMONES "Blitzkrieg Bop"

SALIVA "Ladies and Gentlemen"

NICKELBACK "Rockstar"

SMASH MOUTH "All-Star"

REPUBLICA "Ready to Go"

MUSE "Hysteria"

IGGY POP "Lust For Life"

FATBOY SLIM "Going Out of My Head," "The Rockafeller Skank"

THE KILLERS "Somebody Told Me"

BLUR "Song 2"

WOLFMOTHER "Woman"

3 DOORS DOWN "Kryptonite"

REDNEX "Cotton Eyed Joe"

NEW RADICALS "You Get What You Give"

GNARLS BARKLEY "Crazy"

MOBY "Bodyrock"

CHUMBAWAMBA "Tubthumping"

KERNKRAFT 400 "Zombie Nation"

MP3 Players

Once upon a time, long before the days of iPods, Zunes, the dozens of other MP3 music player varieties and light-weight amplifiers and speakers, amateur DJs used to have to drag around *hundreds* of pounds of sound gear with them to each and every tailgate. With the glut of new audio technology available, packing light and rocking hard is easy. You can leave the multi-disc CD changers at home.

Tailgaters wire up their cars, trucks, vans or RVs to accommodate MP3 players, and have them set to shuffle through a deluxe playlist and pump out the tunes through their installed, vehicle-bound sound system. Others go with more hi- or low-tech options that feature external speaker cabinets, subwoofers and tuner-amplifiers so they can pick up the big game when game time comes.

ESSENTIAL R&B, URBAN CONTEMPORARY AND HIP-HOP TRACKS

BAHA MEN "Who Let the Dogs Out?"

GEORGE CLINTON "Atomic Dog"

USHER "Yeah"

BLACK EYED PEAS "Let's Get it Started," "Don't Phunk with My Heart"

KANYE WEST w/ 50 CENT "Flashing Lights"

SLY & THE FAMILY STONE "Dance to the Music"

KOOL & THE GANG "Jungle Boogie"

NELLY "Ride Wit Me," "Hot in Herre"

NOTORIOUS B.I.G. w/ PUFF DADDY "Mo Money Mo Problems"

HOUSE OF PAIN "Jump Around"

SNOOP DOGG (w/ PHARRELL) "Drop It Like It's Hot"

NAUGHTY BY NATURE "Hip Hop Hooray," "O.P.P."

LL COOL J "Mama Said Knock You Out"

FLO RIDA W/ T-PAIN "Low"

BEASTIE BOYS "(You Gotta) Fight For Your Right," "Sabotage"

SNOOP DOGG (w/ DR. DRE) "Who Am I? (What's My Name?)"

50 CENT "In Da Club"

OHIO PLAYERS "Love Rollercoaster"

EMINEM "Lose Yourself"

Most factory-installed vehicle sound systems don't have wattage to pump out the necessary sound without over-modulating or distorting; replacing your existing car stereo and speakers with a stronger internal amplifier and adding a power subwoofer speaker can help a great deal. But in either case, without an external power source (power inverter, marine battery or generator—covered in the chapter on "Gear") you're bound to put a huge drain on your vehicle battery.

Getting Portable

For those just getting started with a smaller tailgating camp, you might consider the "Portable Outdoor iPod Sound System" with twelve-hour rechargeable battery, cast aluminum body and broadcast-quality microphone like the one that gadget company Hammacher Schlemmer offers. There are inputs with independent volume controls for non-iPod audio devices such as a microphone, guitar, keyboard, or CD player, so you can sing along (karaoke style) or plug in an instrument and play along with your tailgate tunes music. And at twenty-five pounds, this gem isn't much trouble to haul around. www.hammacher.com.

Sirius Satellite and Local "Terrestrial" Sports Radio

If simply cranking up the radio before the big game is less trouble and more appealing, consider the ease of a plug-and-play Sirius Satellite Radio. Many Browns tailgaters have this excellent resource set up alongside their "terrestrial radio" and track the other NFL games in the lots after kickoff (see what hell "Fantasy Football" has wrought?). Sirius offers more than seventy commercial-free channels of music, and regardless of what kind of tunes you're into you'll find some great pregame sounds. Sirius has a contractual relationship with the NFL to broadcast *all* the Sunday games with their "Sirius NFL Sunday Drive" programming. But we can't in good conscience recommend turning off WKNR 850's Mark "Munch" Bishop in the morning hours, or WTAM 1100's Jim Donovan, Doug Dieken and Andre Knott for the Browns game simulcast. Enjoy 'em all. www.sirius.com., www.wtam.com., www.espncleveland.com.

A Note on Game Day "Broadcasting"

Like radio stations governed by the Federal Communications Commission, each amateur and professional DJ has his or her own frequency (read: range) and most DJs go out of their way not to squat on each other's party vibe with their volume and selections. Call it that FCC "zone of reach," if you will—two radio stations on the same frequency being just out of range of each other.

This goes for every amateur DJ. With sound rigs that range from several thousand dollars worth of equipment, right down to the most amateur rocker with a rack unit, boom box and speakers stuffed into the back of the tailgate, every DJ will tell you that the volume is just as important as the choice of tunes. Yet, there is still a degree to which competition is a part of the DJ contingency on Sunday.

"I know there are a lot of 'gourmets' out there.

Honestly, I've never really been a cooking or recipe guy—Roy Maxwell the Brownie Elf is the soup guru at our tailgate. I'm the one cooking with the tunes. That's my party recipe. I love music and I want people to have fun and dance, so to me, hauling out the speakers and picking the right music is critical to keeping the mood up, the spirits high and the people happy. Our tailgate is like a wedding reception on steroids. We really want people to wonder why we have a good crowd. And when people walk by, they get a sense of that from the music we're playing. It really draws people in and puts them in the right mood." —***Dawg Pound Mike Randall***

"ABSOLUTELY CLEVELAND" TRACKS

JOHNNY PEARSON "Heavy Action" (originally theme music for BBC's Superstars series and later for *Monday Night Football*)

SAM SPENCE "Round Up" (NFL Films Theme)

IAN HUNTER "Cleveland Rocks"

EDGAR WINTER GROUP "Free Ride"

JOE WALSH "Rocky Mountain Way"

JAMES GANG "Funk #49," "Walk Away"

BOBBY VINTON "Too Fat Polka"

MYRON FLOREN "Beer Barrel Polka"

FRANKIE YANKOVIC "Who Stole the Keeshka?"

MICHAEL STANLEY BAND "My Town," "Hard Die the Heroes (Masters of the Gridiron)," "In the Heartland"

MOLLY HATCHET "Flirtin' With Disaster"

THIN LIZZY "Jailbreak," "The Boys are Back in Town"

CLEVELAND TUNES "The Browns are in the House"

NEIL DIAMOND "Sweet Caroline"

WAR "Low Rider," "Why Can't We Be Friends?"

BOBBY ST. VINCENT "Sons of the Kardiac Kids"

GREG BARNHILL "Dawg Fever"

BEAU COUP "Born and Raised on Rock and Roll"

FOGHAT "Slowride"

STEVIE RAY VAUGHAN "The House is Rockin'"

KIM CARNES "Somebody Let the Dawgs Out"

THE BLEACHER BUMS "Bernie, Bernie" (the "Louie, Louie" cover)

ELLIOT, WALTER & BENNET "The 12 Days of a Cleveland Browns Christmas"

THE PRESIDENTS OF THE UNITED STATES OF AMERICA "Cleveland Rocks"

Perhaps superfan Dawg Pound Mike—who most would say is on the low-tech end of the tailgate DJ scale with his classic, late '70s/early '80s wooden cabinet speakers—sums up that game day tailgate DJ approach best. Our advice? Try not to blow up your speakers competing with the professionals like DJ Rezinate, Dawg Pound Sound and the handful of others who bring their nightclub-sized gear and spectacle into the Muni Lot to jumpstart the party.

Looking cool is as important as being comfortable. *(Peter Chakerian)*

If the Dawg Pound Sound DJ van is rockin'—and it almost always is—you better come a-knockin'. *(Layne Anderson)*

Customs & Etiquette

"There are a few things to avoid, in my opinion. The biggest thing you shouldn't do is degrade the opposing fans to the point where you look like a terrible fan yourself. Some teasing is par for the course, but a little of that goes a long way. And if you see someone getting out of hand with alcohol, you should try to make sure that you try to help that person and preserve the experience for the other people. Help keep the peace whenever possible, so the police don't need to get involved. Be careful with fire—don't drink too much if you're the one running the campfire or fire pit. And I guess lastly, like the old saying goes, don't be a dick!"
—*Dawg Pound Mike Randall*

There are do's and don'ts for everything from job interviewing to home improvement, and with tailgating, it's no different. These few little important interpersonal tips will go a long way toward making your first (or next) Browns tailgating experience as good as it can possibly be:

DO meet your tailgate neighbors and bring plenty of food and drink to share with them. Starting off on the right foot with them is critical, especially if you like the area you're parked in.

DO bring more food and drink than you might consume so you can share.

DO keep your beverages in opaque (and preferably interesting) cups and vessels, because "Open Containers are Prohibited" and the rules are much different in Cleveland than they are in many other NFL cities across the country, where the parking lots are owned by the team or private companies. 'Nuff said.

DO "pay it forward" with good parking (lot) karma and friendliness . . . in other words, be good to each other. Tailgating is a delicate system and too much pollution (noise, ugly behavior, etc.) wrecks the environment, just like in life. And guys, be *gentlemen*. What would your moms think?

DON'T draw undue attention to yourself or give law enforcement officials a reason to intervene in your tailgate party. This means public intoxication, nudity, etc. The police are cool people; they have a hard enough job to do as it is without you causing them trouble.

> "I remember that about ten years ago, the kids were really rambunctious. There were some horrible fistfights back then, especially with the Pittsburgh Steelers fans. If there's one thing you shouldn't do, it is fight with the opposing fans. I have no ill towards the opposing fans, who are trolling around in their garb before a game. I understand giving them a hard time, I appreciate the rivalry and not 'buddying up' to them, and I appreciate those people loving [their] team, but I don't understand either side hating the other one and thinking it's OK to channel that into fighting [between the] fans. Don't get that at all."
> —*The Taj, superfan from Hudson*

DO give the opposing fans a "hard time" and razz them; you can even call them "assholes" as a part of the now-famous Muni Lot "Asshole Chant" for away fans.

DON'T start *throwing things* at those opposing fans or pick fights with them. No one wants or deserves to be injured, regardless of whom they root for. Leave the physical stuff to the football players with the helmets and pads.

DO be aware that certain locations, like the Muni Lot, are "age-appropriate," as the Taj likes to say. That doesn't mean that the Muni isn't family friendly; it means that families might have some PG-13 type explaining to do of certain behaviors. There's one more reason for you to scope out locations first and determine what spot is right for you and your group.

DO appoint a designated driver and be responsible in alcohol consumption.

DON'T relieve yourself in public . . . or at least where anyone can see. It can get you in some legal trouble. But if you have no other option, or it's an emergency, try to be discreet.

DON'T offer adult beverages to minors or drive under the influence.

> "My motto is, 'Work hard, play hard.' But my advice is, don't get too loaded so that you can't enjoy the tailgate, the food, or you miss the game. There's nothing worse than that. And don't get too big of a vehicle, because it'll be difficult to get into parking places, no matter where you tailgate."
> —*Tony "Mobile Dawg" Schaefer, superfan, Sandusky*

DO be careful with the words "Who Needs Tickets?" For a lot of people tailgating is a preamble to going to the game, but given the number of regular tickets available on game day (none, usually), you don't have many options once you're down there. There are a lot of scalpers in the lots; accordingly, there are also a lot of bogus or counterfeit tickets. If you are going to buy from someone you don't know, it's another case of "buyer beware."

DO choose more legitimate means of acquiring seats if you can help it—be it from season ticket holders, from the Web sites www.stubhub.com (which guarantees the seats sold are real, satisfaction guaranteed) and www.ebay.com (where you can file a grievance if you're unsatisfied).

RETAILGATING

Food & Drink

The "Commissioner of Tailgating" Joe Cahn has been quoted as saying that "Browns fans are a hearty bunch, [a] meat-loving crowd." Truer words were never spoken, but if you spend any time tailgating, you know that pregame meals have long since transcended burgers, hot dogs, brats and deli sandwiches. These days, tailgaters are big into "prep time," cooking on-site and comparing elaborate dishes: ribs, briskets, chicken, chops, pig roasts, lobster bakes, chili, stews, gumbos and dozens of culinary delights.

"The generosity down there is just amazing . . . I have a bona fide doctor, an MD, who brings me something to soothe my throat every time we broadcast. And there are tons of people who bring beverages and snacks and goodies. Honestly, if I ate all the amazing food that people bring to me before every game while we're down there doing the show, I'd easily put on twenty pounds a game—maybe more." *—Mark "Munch" Bishop, sports talk show host, WKNR AM 850*

Photo by Charles Burkett Jr.

"Back when we started, we used to go down there and do hot dogs and beans. It was nothing fancy. But with Fritz and Trapp and the guys I go down with, they pack a [Dodge] Caravan and all the gear goes in and comes out a certain way, you know? Every guy in the group now is in charge of cooking a dinner. I usually bring side dishes, but each guy makes a meal during the season—I'll butterfly steaks, burgers, dogs, eggplant parmesan, stuffed artichokes, peppers and onions and do mussels and chorizo. Some of the other guys have their specialties, too." —*Jim Sgro, Parma*

For the diehard foodies who tailgate, the sky's the limit. And the question "So, what's the secret to your marinade?" is

A Food Network show or tailgate party? Deep fried turkey is just one of the favorites around Thanksgiving in the tailgate lots. *(Layne Anderson)*

So, how does one coordinate a lobster bake for 90 ravenous Browns tailgaters? *Very carefully* and with a lot of planning. *(Layne Anderson)*

just as important to a tailgater as an injury report is to a Fantasy Football participant. What's more, Cleveland is a giant melting pot of cultures—including German, Czech, Polish, Slovenian, Dutch, Latin American, Irish, Italian, British and various Asian cultures—and all have had a hand in forming the city's culture and food. What better way to celebrate such a cultural heritage than through the generous consumption of excellent homemade meals and recipes?

> "We used to spend big bucks once a year and do a high-end gourmet thing with prime rib, scallops and shrimp and stuff during the good weather in the early '90s. Now we have fifteen-twenty people on a good week and we try to keep it pretty consistent in terms of food." —*John Schoger, Lakewood*

> "Our friends start coming at 5:30 in the morning to help put the food together and pack everything up. We usually bring homemade sausage, gravy and biscuits for the morning and work our way into everything from deep-fried Lake Erie perch and walleye to squid and shrimp. I've got a french fryer on my grill,

so we'll also do mushrooms, zucchini, fried macaroni and cheese . . . a lot of people think that is pretty unique." —*Tony "Mobile Dawg" Schaefer, Sandusky*

"Thanksgiving week is just phenomenal now—a total experience. We deep fry turkey and perch, do veggies and onion rings, you name it. There's usually a huge spread on Thanksgiving week down there— stuffed mushrooms, green bean casserole, roast beef, ham, spaghetti with sausage and meatballs, Swedish meatballs, pies and cakes. You get to game time and it's, 'Somebody sell my ticket, I'm too full to go to the game!' I've actually done that before." —*Jim Sgro*

"I remember going to the Salvation Army once looking for one of those 'grandma pots'—you know, blue with the speckles on it. I got one. What I do with it is I take that spicy chorizo sausage out of the skin, I cook it up with a little garlic, and when it's 99 percent cooked up, I drop in a bunch of mussels with the ice and everything and just let them steam. They pop open after steaming away. Then I put it in a bowl

A 2003 survey conducted by Joe Cahn, "The Commissioner of Tailgating," indicated that most tailgaters are between the ages of 25 to 44, and are predominantly college educated men. Of those surveyed 47 percent of tailgate 8+ times a year. Eight home games comprise an NFL team's regular season.

with a piece of bread and you're good to go. The shells almost work like a spoon." —*Jim Sgro*

For Beginners: Making Things Easier on the Meal Front
To the extent you are able to, keep your food situation simple, at least to start. Plan to bring a lot of easy finger-foods, snacks and quick meal items that can be prepared and served beforehand. Go for plenty of variety and, if you have all of these items packed the night before, it will literally take no time at all to have your party up and running.

A "Full Cleveland" Shopping Experience

The Short List for Local Food, Beverages and Provisions
In a cultural melting pot like Cleveland, it's still *way* too easy to just hit your local supermarket. Certainly, these places are a modern marvel and work for convenience. But for a true Cleveland tailgating food experience, you want to be able to commit a portion of your shopping hours on the Friday or Saturday before a Browns game to purchase tailgating treats at these cool, unique specialty locations. Feel free to add your own favorite haunts, restaurants, food co-ops and farmers' markets to the list:

Tailgating Browns fans in San Diego
refer to the city as Dawg Pound West because of all the expatriates and rabid Browns activity there.

Alesci's

4333 Mayfield Rd., South Euclid / 216-382-5100
www.alescifoods.com
One of Cleveland's two great downtown Italian food and
deli markets. Perfect for Old World Italy delights, great sausages, antipasti and killer lasagna.

Azman & Son's Market

6501 Saint Clair Ave. / 216-361-0347
Slovenian favorites including sausage, zelodec, potica and
other delights.

Frank Sterle's Slovenian Country House

1401 East 55th St. / 216-881-4181

Great Lakes Brewing Company

2516 Market Ave. / 216-771-2085
www.greatlakesbrewing.com
The award-winning brewery is always the right choice . . .
and if their limited edition Christmas Ale isn't the official
beverage of late season tailgating, then after all these years,
I wouldn't begin to know what is.

Gust Galluci's Italian Food Market

6610 Euclid Ave. / 216-881-0045
www.gusgallucci.com

Hot Sauce Williams

7815 Carnegie Ave. / 216-391-2230
A great to-go option for the tailgater who isn't into dirtying
the pots and pans or lugging that grill. Great barbecue and
soul food feasts are a short drive from the tailgating lots.

Krusinski's Finest Meat Products

6300 Heisley Ave. / 216-441-0100
Polish treats and spectacular cured meats are the highlight
here.

Marta's Czech & American Restaurant

800 East 222nd St., Euclid / 216-731-9596
www.martasrestaurant.com

Sausage Shoppe
4501 Memphis Ave. / 216-351-5213
www.sausageshoppe.com

Sokolowski's University Inn in Tremont
1201 University Rd. / 216-771-9236
www.sokolowskis.com

Tink Hall
2999 Payne Ave. / 216-696-1717
This large Asian ethnic food market is chock full of everything from dim sum to fresh fish and seafood and all points in between. Overwhelming on a first trip, you should go when you can be focused.

West Side Market
www.westsidemarket.com
How could this be left out of the equation? At the corner of West 25th and Lorain in the Ohio City neighborhood, this Cleveland landmark is a cornucopia of ethnic foods from all over the globe and farm-raised goods from your own backyard.

Fans await a pig roast with all the fixings in the Muni Lot/North Coast Garage quadrant. *(Layne Anderson)*

Other AFC North Flavors

Whether you're a tailgater heading out of town for a Ravens, Bengals or Steelers game, or planning a themed tailgate for one of those match-ups at home, be creative and consider some out-of-town shopping, too. You might not find it in your heart to ever root for their teams, but these cities have dozens of unique food and beverage options at your disposal. Some are merely traditional fare, but others are absolutely great tastes that are not found easily in Cleveland. Please refer to the AFC North guide in an earlier chapter for some hints on what food items could help enhance your themed tailgating experience.

The Browns Tailgating Experience—at Home

How do you capture the essence of tailgating at a home party? It will never be the same, but if you take a page or two (or twenty) out of this book and apply them to your home get-together, you're all set . . . and without having to lug all that gear. Busy families can't always make it to the lots for every home game, but a game day party at home, where you're huddled around the barbecue, the fire pit or the fireplace and HDTV at home, can be a lot of fun, too. The "Perfect Game Plan," if there is such a thing, "all comes down to good people and great times," says Brian Leitch, a tailgating Browns fan from Painesville.

A Few Recipes for Your
C-TOWN TAILGATE

As mentioned earlier, food is a key component to the tail-gating experience as it is with nearly all parties. Here are a few AFC North-themed basics for kicking off your very own tailgate party in the lot or at home:

"FLATTEN THE STEELERS" POTATO PANCAKES

- 6 medium-sized potatoes (peeled, shredded, squeeze excess liquid out)
- 2 eggs (large)
- 1 small onion, grated
- 1½ teaspoons salt
- 1 teaspoon pepper
- 1 teaspoon nutmeg (freshly ground, if possible)
- 1 tablespoon flour
- peanut oil for frying
- sour cream (to taste)

Beat the eggs in a large bowl, and then combine all in-gredients in the bowl, including the potatoes. Heat a skillet to 350° F, then add the oil (about ¼") and let it come to temperature. Take ¼ cup of the potato mixture and drop it into the skillet. Flatten slightly with a spatula, then fry 3–5 minutes on each side until both sides are browned. Can be served with sour cream to taste. Serves 8. Try serving with Mashed Steeler Hash recipe on page 102.

"BEAT CINCINNATI" FIRE-ROASTED CHILI

The Fire-Roasted Part:

- 1 medium red pepper (seeded and chopped into bite-size hunks)
- 1 medium yellow pepper (seeded and chopped into bite-size hunks)
- 1 medium green pepper (prepared same as previous peppers)
- 1 large onion (Bermuda or Mayan sweet, chopped)
- ¼ cup olive oil
- ¼ cup balsamic vinegar
- 1 tablespoon granulated sugar
- salt, pepper and various spices to taste

The Chili Part:

- 1½ lbs. ground chuck
- 1-12 oz. can light red chili beans
- 1-12 oz. can dark red kidney beans
- 1-14.5 oz. can diced, fire-roasted tomatoes
- 2 tablespoons molasses
- 1 tablespoon cocoa
- 2½ tablespoons chili powder
- 2 cloves of garlic (minced . . . prepared garlic is OK)

Fire up your grill to medium-high heat and set your grill basket (see "Gear" section) on the grill to get hot. In a large bowl, pour the oil, vinegar, sugar and spices (oregano, parsley, thyme and sage work well) and whisk together until fully mixed. Place the onions and peppers in the mixture and make sure all pieces are well coated. Spoon vegetables into grill basket, stirring occasionally and baste with spoonfuls of remaining marinade. Once caramelized, scoop the vegetables out of the basket, place in a bowl and allow for cooling.

Brown the ground chuck in a large Dutch oven and add spices. Drain and rinse beans. Add beans, tomatoes (with liquid), molasses, cocoa, chili powder and garlic to the oven. Allow to cook for 3-5 minutes, and then add the cool grilled vegetables and any marinade drippings from the bowl. Simmer chili for up to 1 hour. Serve with your favorite corn bread recipe. Serves 4-6.

"Blast Baltimore" Seafood Chowder

- 1 bag frozen seafood blend
- 1-12 oz. can chopped clams (with broth)
- 1 lb. tilapia (chopped)
- 6 bacon strips (chopped)
- 1 onion (medium, finely chopped)
- 1 carrot (sliced)
- 1 celery stalk (diced)
- 4 cups seafood stock
- 2 cups clam juice (bottled)
- 1 cup white wine
- 2 cups heavy cream or half-and-half
- 2 potatoes (large, diced)
- 1 stick butter (cut into individual pats)
- ½ cup flour
- Juice of 1 lemon (fresh or bottled)
- 2 sprigs fresh thyme
- 1 tablespoon dried tarragon
- 1 bay leaf
- salt, pepper and Old Bay seasoning to taste
- Pepperidge Farm parmesan Goldfish crackers for garnish

In a stockpot on medium-high heat, render the bacon until crisp, and add carrots, celery and onions. Cook until the onions start to get translucent. Add the butter and let cook for 1-2 minutes, stirring briskly. Stir in flour and cook 2-3 more minutes, again stirring briskly. Add the stock, clam juice and white wine. Bring to boil, then reduce heat to medium and let simmer for 10-15 minutes. Add potatoes, cream or half-and-half, tilapia, clams, lemon juice and seasonings. Let cook for another 3-5 minutes, then add the frozen seafood blend and cook for another 5-7 minutes, stirring occasionally. You're ready to go when the shrimp in the pot is a light pink color. Remove bay leaf and thyme sprigs. Serve chowder in a bowl with Goldfish in place of the usual oyster crackers. Serves 4-6.

Mashed Steeler Hash

- 1-12 oz. can of corned beef hash
- 6 eggs (large)
- 6 oz. shredded Mexican cheese
- ½ cup salsa

Lightly oil a large skillet and bring to medium heat. Fry the hash, turning occasionally, allowing the meat-and-potato mixture to brown. Once sufficiently browned, add the eggs (can be leftover-easy or scrambled), salsa and cheese to the skillet. Stir the combination regularly and do not allow it to burn. Serve in a bowl with toast, biscuits, crusty bread or serve over top of the latke/potato pancake recipe on page 99. Serves 4.

"THE FULL CLEVELAND"

- 12 fresh pierogies (preferably fresh, pan fried)
- 1-14 oz can sauerkraut (drained)
- 1½ lbs assorted sausages (kielbasa, bratwurst, etc.)
- Stadium (or other) mustard to taste

Buy your favorite variety of fresh pierogies, panfry them the traditional Cleveland way (in butter) until the turn golden brown. (You can cheat with frozen pierogies if you must, but it's not as good; follow frozen pierogi instructions.) Separately, split the sausages in half and lay them face down on a hot grill or large saucepan. Cook the sausages through, and then add sauerkraut and pierogies to the saucepan. Make sure everything is heated through. Serve with coarse brown mustard or Stadium mustard on individual plates. Serves 4.

BUCKEYE PIE

- ¾ cup creamy peanut butter
- 2 cups whole milk
- 1 large box chocolate instant pudding
- 1-16 oz. package Cool Whip dessert topping
- 4 oz. cream cheese (softened)
- 1 cup powdered sugar
- 2 pre-packaged chocolate pie crusts
- 2-2 cup packages Reese's Peanut Butter Cups
  (rough chopped)

This is a Northeast Ohio classic. In a large bowl, combine peanut butter, powdered sugar and cream cheese, then add 8 oz. of the Cool Whip and whisk until well-mixed. Divide this filling between the two pie crusts. Mix the milk and instant pudding together and allow it to set up a little. Pour the pudding into the two pies (on top of the peanut butter mixture) and spread it evenly. Add remaining Cool Whip on top of the two pies and spread it evenly. Garnish with the chopped Reese's bits and refrigerate until ready to serve. Recipe makes 2 pies, serves 12–16.

A NOTE ON FOOD PREP

As you would with any food preparation, it is essential to ensure "clean cooking" is taking place. Make sure that all surfaces are clean and disinfected before beginning any recipe. Maintain proper food handling according to directions on packaging, cook all meats to appropriate temperatures and keep foods appropriately cold to ensure the elimination of risk for food poisoning, parasites, pathogens and bacteria. Always maintain clean hands, surfaces and utensils while preparing food for your respective tailgate camp and, if transporting food to a destination, make sure to appropriately pack on ice.

RECIPES

The Bloody Mary (a.k.a. the Monday Morning Quarterback)

The words Bloody Mary and tailgating go together like bread and butter, ketchup and mustard. If you want to wow your tailgate crew, try out these specialized recipes. There's an art to the Bloody Mary and no tailgating experience would be complete without one. It's a perfect breakfast accessory and some bars and restaurants have gone so far as to establish their own "Bloody Mary Bar" on Sundays—offering garnishes as varied as salami sticks, crudités and skewered cheese and seafood as a part of this favorite beverage.

Bloody Marys are also a great "hangover helper" (read that somewhere) which make them a great nightcap or end to the afternoon. But how might someone create an AFC North Bloody Mary? All it takes is a little imagination and the willingness to try over and over to perfect the recipe:

The Bloody Raven

- 1½ oz. (or 1 jigger) of premium vodka
- ½ cup Campbell's Tomato Juice
- 2 teaspoons fresh or canned clam juice
- Worcestershire sauce to taste
- fresh horseradish or cocktail sauce to taste
- dash of Old Bay seasoning
- salt and pepper to taste
- garnish with speared shrimp (and/or lemon wedge)

A zippy East Coast treat that offers a nod to the sea fare of Baltimore. Combine the vodka, tomato juice, clam juice, horseradish or cocktail sauce, Worcestershire and Old Bay with 1 cup of ice cubes and shake the mixture well. Strain mixture into a tall glass filled with ice. Garnish the Bloody Mary with a lemon wedge and/or speared shrimp. Toast with an enthusiastic "Modell sucks!"

THE BLOODY BENGAL

- 1½ oz. (or 1 jigger) of premium vodka
- ½ cup V8 juice
- 2 teaspoons fresh or bottled lemon juice
- Worcestershire sauce to taste
- dashes of cocoa powder and chili powder
- celery salt and pepper to taste
- Frank's Louisiana Red Hot sauce to taste
- celery spear and lemon wedge for garnishes

All of the flavors that make Cincinnati chili three-ways flavor this Mary. Follow the directions for the Bloody Raven and serve accordingly. Mock Cincinnati with a hearty Sam Wyche toast ("You *don't* live in Cleveland? We do!") and enjoy.

THE BLOODY STEELER

- 1½ oz. (or 1 jigger) of premium vodka
- ½ cup Mrs. T's Spicy Bloody Mary Mix
- 2 teaspoons fresh or canned sauerkraut juice
- 1 teaspoon of crushed garlic
- Worcestershire sauce to taste
- garlic salt and white pepper to taste
- dill pickle spear for garnish

Follow the directions for the Bloody Raven/Bengal above and serve accordingly. Mock Pittsburgh with a zealous "Pittsburgh sucks!" and enjoy.

RECIPES

The Brownie Mary

- 2 oz. (or 1 generous jigger) of premium tequila
- ½ cup Spicy V8 juice
- 2 teaspoons beef broth or consommé (a dash of beer is a good alternative here, too)
- dash of fresh or bottled lime juice
- Worcestershire sauce to taste
- salt and pepper to taste
- chopped jalapeño to taste
- celery spear and lime wedge for garnishes

Follow the directions for the previous Mary recipes, and offer a "Here we go, Brownies . . . here we go!" before that first sip.

The Brownie BERRY Mary

(for ladies, the diet conscious, and non-Bloody Mary fans)
- 2 oz. (or 1 generous jigger) of premium vodka
- ½ cup V8 Splash Berry Blast
- 2 teaspoons of grenadine syrup
- splash of lemon-lime soda
- dash of fresh or bottled lime juice
- garnish with a lime wedge

Follow the directions for the previous Mary recipes and offer a "Here we go, Brownies, here we go!" before that first sip.

If a Bloody Mary is just not your thing, consider some other party favorites (and hangover "helpers"): an Irish coffee (with Bailey's, Jameson's or Tullamore Dew), or a Michelada (half-beer, half tomato juice with lime juice and salt). Stave off those hangovers with an ice-cold Revive VitaminWater or Gatorade chaser. You can also keep those nasty hangovers at bay by having a glass of water for every adult beverage consumed.

I'm not much of a cook, as anyone who has visited will tell you. I do have one recipe to share, which I call 'Medicine to Ease the Pain of a Browns Loss,' the name coming from an appearance on WMMS. It's equal parts Crown Royal and either regular or diet Mountain Dew. It does the trick, believe me."
— ***The Taj, superfan from Hudson***

Always enjoy your tailgates —home, away and at home— with a designated driver.

Little Brown Riding Hood (left) and Muni the Lot Ness Monster are on the scene at the Muni with a basket full of goodies that probably aren't for Grandma. *(Peter Chakerian)*

THE USUAL SUSPECTS

With all due respect to film director Bryan Singer's crime thriller of the same name, Browns fans should be able to pick *superfans* out in a line-up. If you're a Browns fan you probably know a few hardcore fans yourself. But the odds are, you don't know too many who measure up to *these* diehard tailgate personalities. They fall somewhere in between the recurring "Bill Swerski's Superfans" skit from NBC's *Saturday Night Live*, a riled sports mascot and something out of a DC or Marvel comic book. They're also about as salt-of-the-earth as people come.

These brightly-colored, boisterous boosters and backers of the Browns have supported the team through thick and thin. Nearly all of them would be hard to recognize without their extreme (and sometimes outrageous) attire. They inspire dozens of other fans to embrace their inner fanatic— through dress up, to slathering on make-up and to, as the BoneLady likes to say, "Bone Up."

Some of these "Usual Suspects" fans have a long history rooting for the Browns for twenty years or more and have seen the good, bad and ugly in person; others were inspired to celebrate by the team's return in 1999. All of them have one thing in common: a place to be on Sunday . . . and that's

Photo by Layne Anderson

tailgating. A Sunday spectacle in the Muni Lot just wouldn't be the same without them.

It takes a special kind of creative, devoted person to commit themselves so fully to a caricature and regimen of fandom. So who are these superfans? Read on and you'll learn about a number of them:

TONY "MOBILE DAWG" SCHAEFER

He's a model citizen and the "Custom Tailgate Ride" guy. Contractor and Sandusky native Tony "Mobile Dawg" Schaefer grew up sitting next to his dad at Cleveland Municipal Stadium, watching the legendary running back Jim Brown carrying the ball. It's a memory that continues to fuel Schaefer's superfandom. He joined a coalition of Browns fans and tailgaters in 1995 for the "Save the Browns" campaign (with then Cleveland mayor Michael R. White's office) and later petitioned NFL owners with them after Art Modell moved the team to Baltimore. If not for the efforts of Schaefer and a cast of other superfans who delivered petitions to NFL owners in person, the Browns name and colors might have left town, too. Schaefer is the Master of Ceremonies in the Muni Lot; you can find him and his crew congregated around his "Mobile Dawg Pound". Schaefer's converted school bus is a marvel that features a feisty, peeing "dawg" hood ornament named "Otto" (named after quarterback Otto Graham), a living

"Dawg Pound Mike" Randall (left) and Tony "Mobile Dawg" Schaefer celebrate at an away Browns/Steelers tailgate. *(Layne Anderson)*

The "America's Best Football Tailgating Cities Index" recently ranked

the "tailgating-friendliness" of the thirty-one U.S. cities with an NFL team (plus NFL-hopeful Los Angeles). They ranked AFC North rivals Baltimore #1 and Cincinnati #5, respectively. Cleveland tied Pittsburgh for #18. This ranking focused on "stadium parking lots, overall tailgating environment, tailgating-fan enthusiasm and the sales of tailgating accessories like in-car live TV systems and mobile programming."

room layout and the coup de grace: a porta-potty with Art Modell's face at the bottom of it. Schaefer was elected into the "Visa Hall of Fans" at the Pro Football Hall of Fame in Canton a few years ago and travels to more sporting events every year than most people could manage. He's a salt-of-the-earth guy whose generosity ranges from offering a simple beverage or meal to anyone who comes by, to donating his time and money to charities. On his fanhood: "It's in my blood," Schaefer told Browns247.com. "I will never lose the love I have for the Browns." Find him online at www.mobiledawg.com.

❋ **Little known facts**: Schaefer is a member of the Lake Erie Islands Browns Backers group, loves March Madness and deep-fries the meanest macaroni and cheese you've ever had.

"DAWG POUND MIKE" RANDALL

Randall is "Mr. Congeniality" of the Muni Lot, and that's no slight. Both Randall and longtime Browns Dawg Pound mascot John "Big Dawg" Thompson have taken a lot of grief for not cross-checking or dumping beer on Chad "Ocho Cinco" Johnson when the Cincinnati Bengals receiver leapt up into the Dawg Pound during a home game in 2007. A former member of "Charlie's Fryes," Randall is a marketing professional by day and an Akron native (hence the allegiance to quarterback Charlie Frye while he was a Brown). He's also a Muni Lot staple—a makeshift DJ parked next to Tony "Mobile Dawg" Schaefer's "Mobile Dawg Pound" custom school bus. He attends every Cleveland Browns game, home and away, and you can't miss him in his #1 jersey and unique dog bone hat. Outside of the Muni Lot, you'll find him in the Dawg Pound during games, where he usually takes in the festivities with "Big Dawg." Like Schaefer, Randall is involved with Browns-related activities the year around and has been "attending Browns games ever since childhood." He says being a superfan was never something he aspired to, it just sort of happened: "I'm just a passionate fan who loves the Browns and has a lot of fun with all the added flair." On the Chad Johnson incident: "The negative reaction from some fans was interesting. Do you really think I'm going to lose my Browns tickets and hurt someone? Sorry, but I can't be that guy." You can find Mike online at www. dawgpoundmike.com.

❖ **Little known facts:** His bone hat is a custom lid engineered specifically for him by a Georgia company. He personally hand-painted and sealed it himself.

Layne Anderson

ROY MAXWELL, THE BROWNIE ELF

Maxwell is the ultimate "I Still Hate Modell" fan. Former Browns owner Art Modell was quoted early in his tenure that one of his first official acts was to get rid of the iconic "Brownie Elf" mascot tied to the team's AAFC championship years. It's only fitting that Roy Maxwell, a retired Timken employee, season ticket holder and avid Browns fan would dress for every game as that mascot. After all, Maxwell is the fan who once spelled out "Go to hell, Modell" on a forty-foot-long Christmas light display on his property. Maxwell tailgates with Tony "Mobile Dawg" Schaefer's crew and sports a custom Brownie Elf costume, that was tailor-made for him back in 1999. In previous interviews, Maxwell has delighted in the return of the Elf as a part of the Browns legacy. Scan the Dawg Pound and you'll find Maxwell with a host of other Muni Lot regulars. The soft-spoken guy is pretty unflappable . . . unless you get him started about Modell. "I'm throwing a party in the Muni Lot when he dies, if that tells you anything," he told the Canton *Repository* in the summer of 2005.

❉ **Little known facts:** Maxwell is the "Mobile Dawg Pound" soup guru. "He whips up a different soup every week," says Schaefer. "One time he made a huge batch of this vegetable soup that had, like, fifteen different things in it from his garden. The Elf is always a draw for the police who are working the Muni Lot—especially on those really cold days. They always come down and see what kind of soup he has cooking!"

DEBRA DARNALL (A.K.A. THE BONELADY)

She's a cartoon character come to life and a great example of a "Tailgate Nomad," despite setting up her own camp upon occasion. When you're tailgating in the Muni Lot, you can't miss Debra Darnall. She's the First Lady of the Muni Lot and probably sees the "business end" of more cameras in a week

Walter Novak

than most superfans do. As the BoneLady, she cruises the Muni Lot on Sunday until noon, visiting with fans with a posse in tow. She's been likened to "a character from a John Waters movie" by *Scene* magazine. And for good reason: you can see the BoneLady from a mile away. "I'm a little obsessive, but I'm good with a glue gun," laughs the Lakewood native. "If it makes me laugh, I do it. The first time I dressed up this way, I think I had more fun just watching people's reactions." With her brown and orange dress, giant tchotchke-adorned beehive hat, signature sunglasses and that "Bone Up" blouse, the BoneLady rallies the fans and seems to attract people wherever she goes. And her "BoneMobile" —a classic, colorfully-adorned Volvo station wagon, replete with an eight-foot, illuminated bone—draws just as much attention as she does. Like the many superfans you find in the Muni Lot, she attends nearly every Browns home game in the Dawg Pound, wearing her celebrated garb. She was inducted into the "Visa Hall of Fans" at the Pro Football Hall of Fame in Canton in 2001 and shows no signs of slowing down. "The day it's not fun, I won't do it anymore, but not before then." You can keep up with the BoneLady's schedule online at www.bonelady.com.

❊ **Little known facts:** BoneLady is a professional artist by trade. Her "Bone Up" blouse is not the only mantra you'll find on her body on a given Sunday. Count on her flashing game-appropriate slogans printed on her orange, biker shorts-clad behind: Last year's favorite? (Surprise!) "Steelers Suck."

THE TEMPLE OF THE TAJ

The Taj is a no-frills Browns party animal. If Tony "Mobile Dawg" Schaefer is the Master of Ceremonies in the Muni Lot, then the Grand Marshal, as most fans will tell you, is the Taj. Don't get confused—the Taj is a superfan, but it's also the name of the vintage Tagalong trailer that he resides in during home games. The superfan named the Taj has been a staple in the Muni for over twenty years, although his beginnings were pretty humble: "I've only recently been at the A-Pole consistently. That started in 1999. [Tailgating] started out pretty simply for me: long before I had the camper, I walked around to all the other tailgate parties where my friends were with a bottle under my arm to share." The Taj (along with his friend "Giovanni the Driver") welcomes all fans to come and visit him to talk Browns and to soak up an incessant party vibe that rivals Mardi Gras. The guys parked next to the Taj, collectively known as "Frankenbong" for their beer bong, have a lot to do with how the Taj exists today. "Mark and Al nicknamed the Temple, and they gave me the idea for handing out my orange stickers. Together, we are like the [rock band] AC/DC of our tailgating parking lot. We party it up right, in good weather or bad. If you can't find me, ask someone with one of my orange stickers. By about 10 a.m., they are everywhere!"

The Taj

❇ **Little known facts:** The Taj Temple camper is the only tailgating vehicle specifically identified on a giant mural of the Cleveland Municipal Parking Lot at the Browns training facility in Berea.

THE BRAYLON BUNCH

If the Browns had an official college fraternity, The Braylon Bunch would be it. Members of the Braylon Bunch will tell you their story is an easy thing to explain: they're a popular group of like-minded guys from Cleveland with visions

Layne Anderson

of Super Bowl rings dancing in their heads. Born in a basement in Parma, the Bunch are part Beastie Boys throwback, part football fraternity. The group's name honors the Browns' top 2005 draft pick, Braylon Edwards. You can see (and hear) the Bunch from a mile away—their thumping, super-deluxe orange van includes the group members' photos and retro, *Brady Bunch*-style logo, a beefy sound system and a homemade, hip hop theme-chant-song, "You Know How We Do." The gang runs quite a lot party, known for raucous antics and the "Bunch Bong," a beer bong that services eight people simultaneously and resembles an orange octopus. The Bunch is at their game day best around 11 a.m. You'll have to hit the Muni to know how "Wish," "Anth," "Goof," "Chuckles," "Mar," "Aussie," "Lively" and "T-Balls" rock it on game days.

❋ **Little known facts:** The Bunch helps raise money for Toys for Tots and were dangerously close to being called the "K2 Crew" (in honor of Browns tight end Kellen Winslow, Jr.) when they were formed. That K2 Crew nickname was deep-sixed after Winslow's highly publicized motorcycle accident.

DANIEL RAY PICKEREL

Pickerel is the example of an environmentally conscious tailgater. And yet, he really doesn't tailgate. A "sustainability champ," he's the most regular of the aluminum can collectors in all of downtown Cleveland's lots on Sundays. Thing is, Pickerel is not just a recycling king who cares about the planet; he plays a sport all his own on Sundays: he's an in-line skater who calls his rollerblading on game day "Karmic Hockey" and is said to create bicycles from the cans and other waste products that he collects in the Muni Lot. One thing is certain: the gigantic trash sweepers that troll the Muni and other city lots after Browns games have much less to pick up for his efforts. (Note to fans: if you've never seen those giant sweepers operate long after the fans are gone,

Charles Burkett Jr.

it's a must-watch experience.) Pickerel is certainly not the biggest Browns fan you'll find tailgating, but he's a big fan of Cleveland and that seems to drive him to task every week. Local activist Norm Roulet of the Cleveland-based social online networking site RealNEO.us (http://www.realneo.us) calls Daniel Ray "a modern day St. Francis of Assisi," the patron saint of ecology.

❄ **Little known facts:** Pickerel is a member of the local organization Entrepreneurs for Sustainability, and is big on gardening.

JOHN "BIG DAWG" THOMPSON

The "Superman" of tailgating, "Big Dawg" parlayed his early days in the lots into bona fide celebrity. You can't talk about the Muni Lot without talking about the iconic "Big Dawg". He may be the most famous Browns superfan of all. He is the leader of one of the most famous cheering sections of all time (the Dawg Pound) and has been there since it was christened in 1985 by those lightning-quick Browns cornerbacks, Frank Minnifield and Hanford Dixon. Thompson is usually seen in the Pound in Section 118 with Dawg Pound Mike, and he attends every Browns home game sporting his trademark #98 jersey and iconic dog mask. Astute fans might recall that once upon a time, Thompson was once a much *bigger* Dawg—but has successfully lost a lot of weight and kept it off. A prominent leader of Browns fans, he was a key component of a lobbyist group that helped bring an

Joe "The Commissioner" Cahn's recent tailgater survey indicates that the majority of tailgaters live within an hour of their regular tailgating location, arrive at their tailgating destination three to four hours before the big game; 93 percent of those surveyed prepare their food on site (at the stadium or tailgating lot) and over 85 percent use a grill or a smoker in prepping their grub.

NFL franchise back to Cleveland to assume the colors and heritage. It should come as no surprise to fans that "Big Dawg" has been enshrined in the Pro Football Hall of Fame in Canton as a superfan.

✻ **Little known facts:** Sure, he's been on TV, testified before congress on behalf of the Browns in 1999 and was honored by Rep. Dennis Kucinich. But what you might not know about "Big Dawg" is that he used to be a regular tailgater, too. You're not likely to see him in any of the usual tailgating locations these days (although he's said to still turn up occasionally).

MUNI LOT BROWNS BACKERS, THE REVEREND SCOTT NUNNARI AND THE TAILGATEDAWG.COM CREW

Nunnari's the one guy everyone wants to have at their tailgate and is a classic example of the "Everything and the kitchen sink" tailgater. He's the self-proclaimed "patron saint of partying" in the Muni Lot. The cigar-chomping Columbia Station native and software salesman owns the iconic "DumDog" —a Browns helmet-clad, dog-themed party bus with a giant DirecTV set-up, 20,000 rocking songs on a computerized sound system and plenty of food and drink for all. And if you hang out there long enough, you'll see a steady stream of friends, old and new, stop by to take him up on the party vibe. "That's what's fun about having this bus," he told *Scene* back in 2004. "You meet people every week that you'd never meet." The DumDog insists that you can't miss Nunnari's group— but you could easily look past the Renaissance man him self. Unless he's sporting his requisite orange Santa Claus outfit for the holiday sea-

Walter Novak

son, he usually wears a replica Jim Brown jersey and a ball cap. The bearded "BusDeacon" Nunnari also runs the Muni Lot Browns Backers, a group that is 600 strong and growing. He and his clan—which includes Mark Fielder, Mike Cipalla, Steve Fedorko and Bruce MacLaren—are located in the first section of the Muni Lot, just east of the North Coast garage. www.myspace.com/busdeacon; www.myspace.com/munilotbrownsbackers

❊ **Little known fact:** Nunnari's an ordained minister in the Universal Life Church who has married over a dozen couples in the lot.

BRETT HOLYCROSS

If awards were given out to tailgaters, the Bedford Heights native would win Most Generous Tailgater. He offers ridiculous gourmet feasts to visitors of his RV without asking for a dime. Always anchored in "The Pit" off West 3rd Street in the Flats, Holycross offers up everything from shrimp, fish and chicken to elk, shark, zebra (!) and other wild game. You'll see him dish up food to the homeless, too—a regular occurrence in many tailgating locations.

BROWNS BILLIES

If you hear country music and smell barbecue, you're probably right near them in the Muni Lot. A bunch of self-professed "east side hillbillies" from Chardon, you can spot this rowdy group of fans about mid-lot in the Muni. You can't miss them in their orange "Browns Billies" t-shirts, Browns helmet-painted cowboy hats and cowboy boots. Some of them were spotted in Arizona at the Browns/Cardinals game last year. www.myspace.com/brownsbillies

Layne Anderson

Layne Anderson

CLEVELAND BELIEVERS

Keeping with awards, "Dave," "DJ" and the rest of this Mentor-based tailgating crew wins for "Best DIY Group" on the Muni Lot. Their motto adorns their orange-and-brown Dodge RV: "Never mind the players . . . fear the fans!" You're bound to find them mid-lot, in front of their Dodge, with a spirited game of Beer Pong going. http://www.myspace.com/clevelandbelievers

THE DAWG BROS.

The male counterparts to BoneLady (and seen with her regularly) the Dawg Bros. are "Most Likely to Appear in a Kids' Television Show." Also known as "Bubba Dawg" & "JY Dawg," Joe and Emanual McElwain are a warm, friendly duo from Cleveland's west side, and are on the business end of cameras in the same way their female counterpart is. They're

Walter Novak

part Tonka "Pound Puppies," part Kiss greasepaint and part Mardi Gras in their get-ups. You'll find them in the Muni Lot, fraternizing with fans and other usual suspects.

DAWG FACE DENNY

He's a winner for "Most Old School" if such an award existed for Browns tailgating. A staple of the Muni Lot since the early 1980s, Denny sports a ferocious dog mask, bone decorations and "Dog Face" Browns jersey. Sometimes you'll see him roll up prior to game time on his motorcycle—at least until hunting season. He wears shorts long after it is sane to do so, and parlays his big game hunting into some truly tasty tailgate dishes.

DAWG POUND SOUND

They're a horde of sound-obsessed guys from Toledo who win "Most Likely to Move Your Body." These guys pump out the tunes on a super-deluxe sound system at every home game and get dancers and non-dancers alike rocking. Their white Dawg Pound Sound van, trailer and canopy are a welcome sight in the Muni Lot for all the revelers, who head over to dance and dig their sound. "No one needs sound in our section of the Muni Lot, because they provide it all," laughs the BoneLady. If you hear them, the BoneLady is likely parked close by.

DAWG TALK ISLAND

They win for "Best Regular Joes," hands down. "Hooper" and the gang are a friendly lot and go for a decidedly Put-in-Bay island vibe, celebrating from their bone-clad RV. You can find Hooper and his pals in the Muni Lot and online at www.dawgtalkisland.com and www.myspace.com/delmarva, plotting out their next Browns-related event.

FRANKENBONG

They're "Old School" like Dawg Face Denny, hardcore like the Taj . . . and can give both of them a run for their money, respectively. You'll find Mark and Al—and their freakish beer bong namesake—parked near the A-post, next to the Temple of the Taj in the Muni Lot during every home game. If you're walking the Muni Lot and happen to see a pile of beer cans on the asphalt, look up. They're usually gone come game time. Why? Apparently one of these superfans has been banned from the stadium for life due to conduct. Despite that, you'll never see them miss a tailgate.

FRED THE FRUIT MAN

He wins for "Most Creative Tailgater." Almost always spotted in a Browns jersey, Fred's from Mansfield. If you're having trouble finding him, ask around the Muni Lot for directions because he's a friend to many. Outside of the gourmet nosh he offers to friends and passersby, Fred's real claim to fame? Spirits-soaked pineapple and other fruit bites—hence the nickname.

GARY AND DAWN BROCHETTI

This couple from Euclid wins for "Best Early Bird Tailgating Spot." The duo is usually camped in the Muni Lot long before sun-up, with their giant white canopy against the adjoining North Coast garage. Dawn was instrumental in helping save the Browns with John "Big Dawg" Thompson and Tony "Mobile Dawg" Schaefer, presenting petitions to the NFL owners during a meeting in Atlanta to save the team's name, colors and heritage.

HAWAII BROWNS BACKERS—
HONOLULU CHAPTER

While not technically representing Hawaii, you instantly know where they're coming from. You'll find Jeff and his group give Jimmy Buffett's Parrotheads a run for their money, sporting Hawaiian print shirts, faux palm trees and a cool makeshift tiki bar.

Layne Anderson

MUNI LOT MAFIA

This Stark county group's *Godfather* theme, Italian food-inspired *goomba* nicknames (like Robby Litesauce and Cappy Calzone), and bright orange RV (nicknamed "Good Ol' Sugar") are their claim to fame. "Luca Brazi" may sleep with the fishes, but if the Mafia has anything to say about it, so will the Steelers. www.munilotmafia.com

Layne Anderson

MUNI, THE LOT NESS MONSTER

Playing off the legend/myth of the Lake Erie monster, John Winger is the Muni Lot's answer to the San Diego Chicken. He trolls the lot in a homemade monster outfit to help rally the fans. Friend to all, Muni attracts a lot of the kids and loves posing for photo ops. Occasionally spotted with a sidekick bearing gifts—we'll call her "Little Brown Riding Hood." www.myspace.com/munithelotmonster.

THE BROWNS BOARD TAILGATE

Ed, Don, Stan and the rest of the Browns Board online community are the model "nuts-and-bolts" example of tailgaters—a whole group of well-known superfans . . . without the costumes. For years they have hosted a tailgate before every home game down in the East Bank of the Flats on Old River Road in the parking area between Main Avenue and Front Street. They have fairly large gatherings and have had fans from around the globe attend (over the last couple of years, fans from Europe have landed in their camp). Given the new development occurring on the East Bank, they've relocated to another spot. Keep an eye on www.browns-board.com to find out where they are.

There are literally hundreds of other fans you will see on any given Sunday who live their fandom in exuberant ways. Browse each aisle in the Muni Lot and elsewhere, you're bound to meet many of them—the "Ugly Dawg" gang from Medina, the "Dawg Pound Princess," the nomadic "Super-fan" who arrives by RTA rapid transit and dozens of others dressed as Browns-inspired gauchos, firefighters, chefs, players, etc. The list—and the elaborate costumes and greasepaint—goes on and on. A whole Browns Tailgating yearbook could be devoted to all of these people and their stories.

And knowing how creative these people are, that's probably already in the works.

Many Browns fans and tailgaters have connected with one another

through the Browns Backers Worldwide organization. As of press time, the Backers are nearly 87,000 strong. Visit http://www.clevelandbrowns.com/fans/backers to learn how to join a group near you or organize a new sanctioned group in your town. These groups hold both in- and out-of-season events, tailgates and road trips. As a Browns fan, it's hard not to love a Browns Backers organization once you've joined.

How to be a "Superfan"

Talk to any of the superfans you find tailgating downtown on a Sunday, and they'll tell you a few key things:

★ Being a superfan can be a huge time commitment, as well as an emotional one;

★ Becoming a recognizable figure like the ones profiled can be a long, ongoing and organic process. Don't expect camera crews and media attention. And if either happens, it won't be overnight;

★ Do what you like to do and have a thick skin about it . . . because not everyone who loves football or loves the fans necessarily loves a superfan. Expect the same heckling and razzing that stand-up comics (and some opposing fans) get;

★ Be an original, enjoy yourself, have fun and explore your creativity;

★ Beyond the first four pointers, do it for all of the right reasons—not for the money and attention that other fans think you're getting out of the deal.

The BoneLady breaks it down for any fan considering crossing the threshold to superfandom:

"I try to do as much good things with the popularity. I do charity work, spend a lot of time with kids in the Muni Lot and try to use my profile to draw attention to important things. What's amazing is just how many people are interested in the BoneLady and how important seeing me down there has become to them as a part of their experience. I guess I didn't realize that until more recently. I actually had a couple invite me to their wedding and I didn't know who they were—but it meant that much to them.

"I just don't drink on game day. I don't want to be 'Bad Santa,' you know? I'm representing women in the Pro Football Hall of Fame in Canton as a fan, which is a very big deal to me. And I take that really very seriously.

"There are some drawbacks, which are minor to me and I wouldn't trade what I do for anything. But expectations have definitely changed my game day experience. If I went down there as Debra, it would be different. That goes with the territory. People might say, 'Quit doing it,' but I won't because it's fun and I put a smile on the faces of a lot of people. If I can do that on a Sunday afternoon, I will do it. When a little kid runs up and hugs you, I've got to say that's the best." —*The BoneLady, superfan from Lakewood*

Dawg Pound Mike agrees, offering similar pointers for those who might consider the mantle of superfandom:

"You need to be in it for all the right reasons— because you're a fan of the team who feels passionately about the team. It's about getting close to the fans, having fun and not asking anything in return. As a result, you can help draw attention to issues and help charities, too. But for some people, [becoming a superfan] is just a gimmick to attempt to sell merchandise and draw attention.

"Do whatever your heart feels and do whatever you feel strong about. But have a thick skin about

it, because some fans will think you're in it for the money . . . question your fanhood, or say that I'm paid by the Browns—which isn't true at all. We all pay for our seats and tailgating is totally worth it to us. It's our vice, that's our buzz, going to a game and being a part of the atmosphere. Anytime you put yourself out there, you're going to get harassed. It comes with the territory."
—**Dawg Pound Mike Randall, superfan from Akron**

The BoneLady has her own message for people considering a move to the outlandish costumes and persona of superfandom:

"Ask yourself what the motivation is. If you want to do this for fun, then do it. If you have an agenda, if you're trying to do it for money, for the celebrity or notoriety, for the X, Y and Z, then don't do it. It's fun for me and has taken on a life of its own and I don't care what other people think about it. If I would have listened to every person who told me I was crazy for painting up my car, dressing up like this and doing what I've felt compelled to do by all those negative people, I would have missed out on the best friends I have in my life today. Life is short. You can't worry about what other people think." —**The BoneLady**

PARKING CLAIM CHECK

250-244

Standard Parking

THIS CONTRACT LIMITS OUR LIABILITY- PLEASE READ IT
This parking ticket is your parking contract. This contract limits our liability. It licenses you to park one vehicle in a designated area at your sole risk and at posted rates. Any car parked at this facility is parked at the car owner's sole risk.
OPERATOR does not guard or assume care, custody or control of your vehicle or its contents and is not responsible for fire, theft, damage or loss. The owner alone is responsible for parking and locking his car. OPERATOR issues this ticket as your contract and for timekeeping purposes only. Only a license to park is granted hereby and no payment is
claim check. This is your

Tailgate Rides

One tailgating trend that has emerged over the last several years is the notion of the "Tailgate Ride." Modern tailgating incorporates acres of vans, pickup trucks and sport utility vehicles; all have the ability to haul more of the comforts of home than the usual passenger car. And you've never seen anything like it when all of these vehicles are lined up together. Bring your average auto enthusiast down to the parking lots on a Sunday and, even if they're not big on the Browns or tailgating, you'll impress them with the variety (and creativity) of the "tricked-out," themed vehicles and their amenities.

You can't miss the BoneLady's bright orange Volvo in the Muni Lot, jam-packed with bumper stickers and a giant bone mounted on the roof. *(Layne Anderson)*

"I have some good friends who are the classic tailgaters—they leave as early 6 a.m. for those prime spots in the Muni Lot. They are always alternating who's cooking and what's on the menu. They used to own a used, jalopy Checker Cab limo and painted it to look like a Browns helmet. It could hold about twelve people. I think it crapped out on them finally; they had it for two years and did as much restoration as they could without spending a lot of money on it. I see a lot of those kinds of vehicles coming in to cover a game on Sunday."
—*Tony Grossi,* **Plain Dealer** *Browns beat reporter*

But truly hardcore tailgaters are "tricking out" their rides like never before—with everything from high-definition television, satellite dishes and custom bars, to full-blown living and sleeping quarters. And that says nothing of the amazingly creative paint jobs and decoration adorning them.

"My buddy and I decided that because of the lack of facilities that were in the lot we tailgate at—at the corner of West 3rd and Summit on the high side under the bridge—having a motor home would be a good idea. It's worked out nice having a bathroom, a grill and all the amenities with us. This one is a 'plain Jane' stock motor home, but we've thought about customizing it every time we see another one painted up. When we upgrade to a newer model, we'll definitely be interested in painting that up." —*Bob Geiger, Bay Village*

Motorhomes
Matt Edwards's "Brownzilla" sits atop the high end of tailgate rides for Cleveland Browns tailgaters. The full-length land cruiser sports the license plate "BRNSRV" and features

dozens of larger-than-life vinyl decals of famed Browns players in action on the sides. One side features legendary Browns players (like Bernie Kosar, Kevin Mack, Otto Graham, etc.) with more recent Browns players in action shots on the other side.

A member of the Akron Browns Backers, Edwards says that he and several of his friends have tailgated to Browns games for many years. The idea for Brownzilla came when Edwards purchased the motor home. Not content to leave it plain, one of his good friends—who works at a facility that fabricates shrink-wraps for advertising on public transportation—took on the task of shrink-wrapping the entire motor home. When he and his tailgating pals arrive in the Muni Lot, they're able to bring *everything* with them and arrive in the lot in style.

Busses

Scott Nunnari's "DumDawg" is perhaps the most recognizable vehicle in the Muni Lot, with a design that falls somewhere in between cartoon caricature and outlandish, drug-induced hallucination. With a cabin that resembles a giant, helmet-clad dawg head biting down on a cask of brew, the DumDawg is part of the caravan that Nunnari, the Muni Lot Browns Backers and the Tailgatedawg.com crew assemble in the lot for every home game.

Nunnari's bus has morphed over the years, starting out with a rather plain exterior and benefiting from regular elbow grease and a passion for Cleveland Browns football. Now decked out to the nines, it features more than just a spectacular exterior design. With satellite television, a great sound system, spectacular sports bar layout with classic memorabilia and signatures, the bus has room for at least a dozen or more tailgaters inside.

Stick your head inside and you might think you're looking at a mobile Cleveland Browns Hall of Fame. Oh, did

"It's Alllliiiiiveeee!" The Brownzilla Mobile Home dwarfs everything in its midst. (Matt Edwards)

The DumDawg Megabus party vehicle is a fully-loaded conversion—a Muni Lot staple with big effect. (Layne Anderson)

Tony "Mobile Dawg" Schaefer's "Mobile Dawg Pound." (Peter Chakerian)

I mention that the DumDawg regularly "lifts its leg" on a Pittsburgh Steelers fire hydrant parked next to it?

Another one of the "Usual Suspects," **Tony Schaefer's "Mobile Dawg Pound"** is yet another converted bus—a school bus turned RV that features a living room, a port-a-potty with former Browns owner Art Modell's face at the bottom of it and room for several of his tailgating posse. Similarly adorned with signatures and Browns memorabilia, the "Mobile Dawg Pound" is like most of the tailgating vehicles out there—it had very humble beginnings and came to its current shape with long days of hard work.

> "We bought the current [Mobile Dawg] bus up in Toledo, where they sell buses of all sizes. We had about sixty different ones to choose from; there were maybe five or six that I liked. I had a group of friends and a mechanic look them over before we bought it. From there, my sons Ray and Tony were the inspiration. We all did the auto work, sandblasted it and hand painted it ourselves. Just redid it three or four years ago, and had the decals applied that you see now. But the inside . . . the signatures are all genuine." *— Tony "Mobile Dawg" Schaefer, superfan from Sandusky*

Edwards, Nunnari and Schaefer are but three examples of the hundreds of tailgaters who have taken their fandom to a whole new level with their Browns vehicles.

Tony "Mobile Dawg" Schaefer's Art Modell toilet in his Mobile Dawg Pound conversion bus. No "number twos" allowed. *(Layne Anderson)*

Like everything else they do on game day, these tailgate vehicle owners are original and anything but ordinary . . . and pictures of these and other tailgate rides reflect that.

"We've got forty-two signatures. I think the best story on the signatures came from the expansion draft we drove to in Canton. When we arrived, [security] had us pull up front when we arrived. Afterward, when we came outside, there was a limo parked behind us. We were all laughing, 'That must be someone important!' And sure enough, out came Al Lerner and Carmen Policy. My son asked if they would come into the Mobile Dawg Pound and they agreed. They looked it over and thought it was pretty cool— even the Art Modell toilet—and they both signed it. We've got [Bernie] Kosar, [General Manager] Phil [Savage] and [Coach] Romeo [Crennel], and [owner] Randy [Lerner], too. I swear, I never thought I'd get [running back] Jimmy Brown on the bus to sign it. But he did. That was a dream come true.

"When the team came back, I decided to get a newer and much bigger bus, because our group of season ticket holders out in Sandusky doubled. I had been getting a lot of attention in the media and had been the Reiter Dairy 'Fan of the Year,' and on [WUAB-TV] Channel 43, but I didn't really have a nickname. That's when someone in our group told me I should go with the nickname 'Mobile Dawg' because I was traveling to four or five away games a year. It all just sort of happened; it wasn't anything I planned to do. I'm just a huge Browns fan."
—*Tony "Mobile Dawg" Schaefer*

The "Old School" bus owned by John Schoger and friends. Characters like Speed Racer, Chief Wahoo, the Brownie Elf and others are painted on the windows. *(Layne Anderson)*

A Muni Lot legend: The Temple of the Taj *(Peter Chakerian)*

A converted hearse sports the Brownie Elf in the Naval Lot *(Layne Anderson)*

Kickin' It "Old School"

Lakewood resident John Schoger's school bus conversion is called **"Old School,"** and on the scale of discretionary spending, he started out on the low end. He paid less for Old School than most people do to have their brakes done: "With an old bus, you get a lot for your money, and a lot of them are being scrapped these days—what a waste! A guy I know at work was getting rid of a church bus. It was perfect timing—we bought it in the spring and had all summer to work on it. It's the best $500 I ever spent."

Schoger's vehicle is very much a work in progress—with custom painting, caricatures and flames on the back done by amateur artist Cyndy Mrazeck. Most of the structural work ("all the cutting and body welding") was done by his son-in-law, Tom Stein. The other people in his tailgate group— friends Bucky Stover, Marvin Ruggles, Don Nelson, Steve Kmetz and Tony Acerno—have all helped with the bus.

Future plans for expanding Old School include "putting a second level on her—a raised railing and a deck with a round staircase to get up there, if you will. I have some really bizarre plans for it. But we're still in the planning stages. Laugh if you will, people laughed when I bought the bus."

"Our ride is like an outdoor patio living room in the back. You could compare it to people pulling up with their vans and cars with their trunks open. We've got a huge trunk that opens, too. Except that it's bigger, badder, better. My original concept was to cut the whole back half of the bus and leave it like an open air terrace. But I've never cut a bus open before and once we started, it was a lot more involved than we thought. We went with the removable glass sections in the back and put the couches back there to give Old School a more open-air porch atmosphere."
—*John Schoger, Lakewood*

Campers and the Tailgate Taj Mahal

Campers are a common site in the parking lots across the North Coast on a Sunday. You'll see a fair number of fifth wheel campers, pop-ups and an occasional "tagalong" camper. But you'll never see anything quite like Hudson superfan The Taj's "Temple of the Tailgater." While not exactly a cutting-edge ride, "well-loved" doesn't even begin to describe it:

> "There have been three versions of The Taj. The original trailer was a tagalong trailer from 1960. The name 'The Taj' came from my neighbors in the lot, Mark and Al, who have the Frankenbong. [Mark] came over and called it the 'tajalong,' then that became the Taj Mahal, and before you know it, me and the trailer were both nicknamed 'The Taj.' The Frankenbong guys named me. When the game starts, it's almost depressing to me even though I'm a huge Browns fan and always will be. For me, I'm all about the party and I miss having all the people around. We're all steadfast fans of the team, but to me, it's all about the party, win or lose."
> —*The Taj, superfan from Hudson*

The curremt Taj (the trailer) is the fourth of its kind. With the most recent one, the Taj commissioned an artist to start painting pictures of fans on it. "If you make it to twelve games in a row, and you visit me each time, I take your picture and [the artist] paints your caricature on The Taj." Why? "I do it because tailgating is all about the fans, even more so than the Browns. That's why the trailer is called 'The Temple of the Tailgater.'"

Cars, Trucks, Vans and Livery Vehicles

Superfans Dawg Pound Mike Randall and the BoneLady

have fairly high-profile cars that have been customized to reflect their allegiance to the Browns. You simply can't miss their rides. But they're not the only ones making a statement with their transportation.

> "I'd say the BoneMobile—which is a 1987 Volvo 240—has about 250,000 miles or more on it. It's a Volvo, you know? Not to turn this into a commercial, but I know people who have 400,000 miles on their Volvos. You can drive them forever."
> —*The BoneLady, superfan from Lakewood*

Troll any of the parking lots and you'll see some truly amazing things—from the mid-1960s white hearse and Brownie Elf limousine, to the converted Put-in-Bay "Tailgate Response Unit" ambulance and dozens of brown-and-orange sedans, coupes, conversion vans and others. Some are fairly intricately done and immaculately kept; others,

"Sik Dawg" is a decommissioned Put-in-Bay ambulance found by a Northeast Ohio couple on eBay, then converted to a *party* wagon. (Peter Chakerian)

like the signed Browns van owned by Brian Leitch and Laura Hlebak from Painesville, are straightforward—sufficiently broken in, basic and well-loved. And that's exactly how they like it.

> "We've been tailgating for about four years now and have always been big fans—my nephew Chris had season tickets and started going down and that lured us down there. This other couple went in halves with Laura and me and we bought the van we come down in now. We paid $200 for the van in to- tal—$50 from each of the four of us. Then the other couple signed it over to us as a birthday present. It was pre-painted and we took the bench seat in the back out, put in some Astroturf, built a platform and then we built a bed in the back for camping. We did it because sleeping in the front seats down [in the Muni Lot] that first year that Saturday night before the first game of the season absolutely sucked. We just fixed a few things, added the marine air horn and some other things . . . threw the grill in the van, grabbed some beers and just went down." *—**Brian Leitch, Painesville***

Brian Leitch (left) and Laura Hlebak enjoy a quiet moment in their Browns helmet–painted minivan. It has Astroturf and bunks for sleeping. *(Layne Anderson)*

Finding Brian and Laura in the Muni Lot is a fairly easy proposition: listen for a piercing boat air horn, then look for the orange van with Browns drapes on the windows and a slew of Browns player signatures scrawled all over it.

Other Wild Rides

Keep your eyes peeled. A quick scan of your lot is likely to yield a whole host of other crazy vehicles—from "cooler cruisers," mini bikes and mopeds to the Cleveland Browns "Go Couch." (That's right, a *mobile couch*). In the Muni Lot, a group of ragtag tailgaters cruise the aisles on a nine-foot itinerant sofa that has been mounted on a tractor chassis and cab suspension system. And if you're a cute gal, the varying number of mostly male drivers are more than happy to give you a lift from one part of the lot to another.

Need a lift? The venerable Browns "Go Couch" in action. And yes, the attractive ladies get first dibs. *(Charles Burkett Jr.)*

A Browns helmet-inspired mini-motorcycle and driver cruise the Muni, looking for the next party.
(Layne Anderson)

Creating Your Own Tailgate Ride

Need some tips for creating your own customized ride? If you're looking to tailgate in a specialized vehicle during Browns season, it helps to figure out just what you're hoping to achieve with it. Do you want it to be a functional party vehicle, or a conversational art piece just for show? And what are you looking to spend on it? Choosing which variety of vehicle you want to use for tailgating can take some thought and ingenuity.

First decide what kind of vehicle you're after, then set yourself a budget and start trolling the used car ads in the newspaper and online. Check out eBay as well. When you find the right vehicle, find a good mechanic or handy family member who loves working on cars and have them check out the vehicle you're thinking about buying. Then after all that, get creative.

Here are some other tips:

- Set yourself a budget and stick to it. You don't have to be rich to have a super cool tailgate ride, but you could easily spend more than you planned if your eyes get bigger than your wallet.

- Consider a larger vehicle. You might have a small tailgating group to start, but if your group and camp grow over time, you'll need the room to transport more people, food, beverages and equipment. Size, as they say, really does matter. If one of your tailgating pals has to ride "shotgun" with your grill between his legs on the way down to Cleveland Browns Stadium, you might think about a larger vehicle.

"Make the effort to find a good, solid and inexpensive vehicle. Fix it up right, take your time with it and do it right. Make sure you have a lot of help, because it will be more work than it looks. When you're piecing everything together, make sure it's respectfully done for the team, the fans and the NFL. Get your tailgating friends to put a lot of elbow grease and help you keep it going."
—*Tony "Mobile Dawg" Schaefer*

- Pick a vehicle with "good bones." You want something structurally sound and safe, but not just for the safety of you and your crew. If you have any plans to customize the vehicle—e.g., altering the arrangement of the interior, adding a souped-up sound system, television, bar, bathroom or appliances—you'll need it to pass muster in a vehicle inspection.

"We took a bunch of seats out, put in a bed, table, a fridge and our Art Modell toilet. My sons have used the bus for their high school proms, for homecomings and they used it in their weddings. You can get eight to ten couples in it; we know for a fact you can get a whole wedding party in there." —*Tony "Mobile Dawg" Schaefer*

- Plan on having extra juice. Power adapters, marine batteries, generators and other power sources are important if you plan on running an HDTV with satellite, refrigerator and a handful of other items during your tailgate. Your vehicle's battery shouldn't be compromised by these trappings and accessories.

BROWNS TAILGATING STORIES

Everyone has them—stories that get passed along among family and friends, from generation to generation. Tales and memories from life experiences that often take on a life all their own when delivered in social situations.

Remember where you were during the best and worst of times? On the hottest and coldest days on record? Those incredibly tall tales—hysterically crazy circumstances that are so outlandish and unbelievable that they are movie-worthy? Those sad, "Where were you when . . . ?" moments that are shared in reference to national and global tragedies.

We all do it. And who better to know trauma and share stories about it than tailgating Browns fans?

In the psychology of sports, there's little doubt that sharing stories is a coping mechanism for dealing with staggering loss . . . but it also lends to the healing process and leads to those urban legends that enhance the overall experience of all tailgaters and sports fans. These stories become icebreakers, the basis for conversations and really are a medium of entertainment all by themselves.

In the Muni Lot, costumes are all the rage.
Horse and buggy? Not so much.
(Layne Anderson)

For people who grew up in Cleveland during the 1960s and 1970s, you know there wasn't much to be proud of in town except the Browns. Fans wear their game day and tailgate experiences like a badge of honor, with a sense of pride, attachment and attitude that you just don't see in fans of other NFL teams. "It goes way beyond the game. It's in your blood," says the BoneLady. And she's right. Game day moments are seminal experiences—they stick with you and never fade.

Hang around long enough and you'll hear these stories every week, shared between fans in the lot. You'll hear the stories about the best and the worst of times, the glory of the big games, and the humanity of those painful losses. You'll get firsthand accounts of "The Drive," "The Fumble," "Red Right 88," "The Helmet," "Bottlegate," and hundreds of smaller stories that might never make it to the greater collective consciousness in the lots. It can be an eye-opening experience.

Tailgating Browns fans' stories, reflections and memories are among the richest in the NFL. Here are but a handful of them to enjoy. While by no means a comprehensive overview or true timeline from the tailgate community, it's a great stepping-off point for sharing your own game day tailgating memories with others around you.

The Best of Times

More often than not, Browns tailgaters will tell you that the experience prior to game time regularly eclipses the game itself. Certainly that has a lot to do with the heartbreak associated with the team's painful losses, but tailgating has always been about the party and personal connection. Ask around the lots and you'll find that connecting to family and friends, specific in-lot fun and overall excitement and the specter of a possible playoff success make for the greatest tailgate memories.

> "The best memories for me are when we made the playoffs in the '80s and the Muni Lot was full—and I mean absolutely packed—by 6:30 in the morning. It was bursting and the love was overflowing, and all before breakfast time! It hasn't been that way for a long, long while. When we get back to the playoffs, you'll have to be there by 5:30 a.m. to make sure you get in. At least 5:30. Maybe even earlier."
> —*The Taj, superfan, Hudson*

> "This year [2007] was one of the most exciting years for me, with seven home wins. But I think the most memorable moments I have tailgating have been of my son growing up down there. He's been able to have a great time, meet new people and have the whole experience of tailgating since he was nine or ten years old. He's met the parents of some players being down there with all our friends Browns players down there as well. His room is painted orange with the brown stripe and [he] has Browns memorabilia all

over. It's important to him, and an opportunity we'll both never forget." —**Bob Geiger, Bay Village**

"Sometimes it's tough. I can't point to a specific memory from tailgating that stands out because they're all great. I'd say there have been so many Muni Lot parties, no one could be better than the others because they're all so damn much fun!" —**Tony "Mobile Dawg" Schaefer, superfan, Sandusky**

"I think the first time staying overnight in the Muni Lot was big. It was Ohio State's first game that Saturday and we had a satellite dish, a generator, and a projection TV and watched [that game] on the side of the van. About two dozen people ended up watching that OSU game down there, all the people in a big huge horseshoe around the screen. Next year, it seemed like everyone started doing that." —**Laura Hlebak, Painesville**

"I grew up in a family where we didn't go every week, but we made sure that the week we did go, we had a blast. It's fun. I've enjoyed being a part of the Sunday tradition, going down with my father and uncles. I remember that first beer that I had down there [that] you're not allowed to have. We'd be down at the Muni Lot most of the time, and after you go for so long, you just know people from there even if you don't talk to them all year long. We had friends who worked at Goodyear and Firestone back in Akron who would go down, too. They worked hard and on Sundays, these hardcore, tough workers were having a great weekend away. The Browns game was their opportunity to have a good time. I'll never forget those times, that fun and those conversations down there." —*Andre Knott, WTAM 1100 Browns beat reporter*

"We've had four different couples meet at the Taj who have come back to our tailgate to get married. Those are some pretty cool memories—that people who met there at my trailer are now married. For the last one, BoneLady and I were the maid of honor and best man. And yes, the couples are all are still married and come back and visit. I think that going to tailgate can be a great place to meet people and I think those weddings prove it." —*The Taj*

The Worst of Times

As fans of the Browns, we all wear our hearts on our collective sleeves, bleed orange and brown and know a thing or two about heartbreak and disappointment. Whether it's "The Drive," "The Fumble," "Red Right 88," "The Helmet" or "Bottlegate," odds are, you have your own feelings tied to a specific Browns event. For tailgaters, those feelings don't simply get turned off like a television set. They spill over into the lots *after* the game.

"I think 'The Drive' was one of the worst ones I can remember experiencing as a tailgater. Being down there for that was just heartbreaking; everyone was just so depressed. There have been other times where things felt pretty bad down there. There was that Kansas City game where [Browns linebacker]

Dwayne Rudd threw his helmet and got the un-sportsmanlike conduct penalty that led to a field goal and a loss. That was rough, too. And there was that Christmas Eve when we got blown out by the Pitts-burgh Steelers. You might have been mad watching the game from home, but you really have no idea how hard the tailgaters take it unless you're down there watching." *—Tony "Mobile Dawg" Schaefer*

Eternal optimists that we all are, we won't belabor the point about the losses and heartbreak. It certainly is a big part of who we are, but hey, the Browns are going to the Super Bowl this year, right? Perhaps talking about the worst of times in the parking lots as it relates to weather will brighten the mood:

"My dad and I went to this incredibly cold Browns/Minnesota Vikings game in the late '80s. Man, it was cold as all hell and I remember my mom say-ing to both of us, 'I don't think it's smart to go down there,' blah blah blah. Turns out she was right: my dad and I froze our butts off, but we both stayed for the tailgate and the game. He didn't want to admit to me he was cold, I didn't want to admit it, either. Both of us didn't want to go home to hear it, but we were dying! But being manly, and having this father-son bonding experience, neither one of us wanted to admit we were cold. We both got home and it was funny because we were both being so tough about the whole thing. These days, I look at everything dif-ferently, being thirty years old and having the gig I do, but that has not changed how I see [tailgating]." *—Andre Knott*

"For all the years and bad weather, I've never seen anything quite like the Buffalo game in December of 2007. You could talk about that December 2004 San Diego [Chargers] game or the Browns/Raiders AFC playoff in '81, but for that Buffalo game, the snow was coming at you like it was coming out of a cannon. The first hour was pleasant enough, but near the end of the broadcast, we had rigged up some sides to our open canopy, had a second tent pitched to buffer the wind and had four crew members holding the tent down to keep it from it blowing away." —*Mark "Munch" Bishop, sports talk show host, WKNR AM 850*

"The coldest game for me was the *Monday Night Football* game against the [St. Louis] Rams [on December 8, 2003]. We had a wedding at the Taj that day. It wasn't that cold, but we started in the Muni Lot very early, and we were at the WMMS studios for the bachelor party for a little while before we got back to the Muni Lot by noon. Then we were partying the whole rest of the day. I only vaguely remember being cold sometime mid-afternoon; I had only been wearing a sweatshirt around and it was ten degrees or something. That was a bruiser for me." —*The Taj*

In the 1970s and '80s, concertgoers would camp outside and tailgate overnight at Cleveland Municipal Stadium. With limited provisions and without their cars, they plunked themselves down in front of Gate E, waiting for tickets to go on sale. The author recalls waiting for tickets to see The Who, the Rolling Stones and Pink Floyd that way.

"Last year, Buffalo was the one that took the cake. We weren't going to even drag our bus 'Old School' down there, because we were worried about it starting and running. But everyone in our group said 'We've got six wins in a row when we bring it down, we have to take it.' I think we spent a half-hour cleaning the blizzard out of the cockpit, because someone left the back door opened an inch. It was only an inch, but you wouldn't believe how much snow got in there!" —***John Schoger, Lakewood***

Everyone remembers their worst bad weather day. Personally, the game we played against San Diego in 2004 tops the list . . . and the Muni Lot was definitely still hopping. Those are the days that hardcore fans love to relive in a conversational circle—when you need beer for your insides and hot coffee to pour on your fingers and toes, just to keep them

Three words. Orange helmet hair. *(Peter Chakerian)*

from freezing. Those are the kinds of days that tailgaters tell their kids about.

On December 19, 2004, the conditions included a game time high temperature of 18 degrees (-10 with the wind chill factor) and snow flurries and squalls. The Chargers defeated Cleveland 21-0. The coldest Browns home game (and one of the Top 10 coldest NFL games on record) took place at Cleveland Municipal Stadium on January 4, 1981 in the AFC playoff game between the Browns and the Oakland Raiders. The temperature that day? Five degrees below zero.

> "When the weather is crappy here, it becomes part of the mystique and a topic for fans to debate, 'Which game was colder?' I remember talking to [the late Cleveland sportscaster] Pete Franklin when he left here for San Francisco and he told me that [California] 'could never be close to the same as Cleveland. People there go to mountains or the beach, the weather is beautiful and Lake Erie will never be Big Sur. But the fans out there don't even compare to ours.'" —*Terry Pluto,* **Plain Dealer** *sports columnist*

Wild and Crazy Stories

Best and worst times aside, the wild and crazy experiences in the parking lots are often the ones that live on long after any tailgate experience. Those legends and anecdotes take on a life of their own as they're told and retold to friends and newcomers. They become a part of the fabric that binds people together. In my time tailgating, I've seen some incredible things, including a rather inebriated Browns fan being physically attacked by his girlfriend for his attempts to pick fights with others. I've seen rambunctious Pittsburgh Steelers fans have their own tailgating vehicle (parked in the Muni Lot) "shrink-wrapped" with cellophane and covered with food. I've seen groups of people racing "cruiser coolers," line dancing and break dancing. And I've seen full pig roasts and lobster bakes for 100 people that weren't catered.

Head to one of the lots on a Sunday and you'll see some pretty amazing things to report back to your family, friends, co-workers and anyone else who will listen. Here are just a few stories to whet your appetite:

> "You see all kinds of crazy stuff down at the Muni Lot. I remember one time down there before a Steelers game, back when Neil O'Donnell was the quarterback and before the Browns moved. I was down there getting ready to do a report and these guys who had this beat-up RV pulled me aside and said, 'You gotta check this out!' They had built this giant wooden outhouse in the lot—eight feet tall by four feet wide—but when you opened the toilet inside, it was a fake: they had built a little ledge with a toilet seat, but when you opened the cover, there was a picture of Neil O'Donnell's face on the inside. It wasn't a fully functional toilet. But I remember going back to those guys when I had my cameraman with me an hour later, and here people had actually started using the fake outhouse without the plumbing. When I opened the door, the aroma almost knocked me over. Still to this day, I think the O'Donnell outhouse was one of the wildest things I witnessed down there." —*Tony Rizzo, WJW-FOX 8 sports anchor and WKNR-AM broadcaster*

Truer words never were spoken.
For the 2007 NFL Fan Value Experience survey, the *Sports Illustrated*
Web site concluded that the Cleveland Browns game day crowd "is
knowledgeable and loud, as well as profane, inebriated and obnox-
ious." It adds that fans are "very intense" but "sometimes not suit-
able for individuals under the age of 18."

"The first time we went down with the van, we had
an inverter and marine batteries and everything was
all set up to the satellite dish we had and then the
TV we brought didn't work. So what did we do?
Went to our next door neighbors in the lot, asked
if they had an extra TV and they said they weren't
watching it and to go ahead and borrow it. In the old
days, you'd borrow a cup of sugar from your next
door neighbor in your town. I was thinking to myself,
'Where on earth could you go and meet a thousand
perfect strangers, ask to borrow a TV from someone
. . . and they actually had one to lend and said yes,'
you know? You couldn't do that with your neighbors
in your own neighborhood, but you could do it in the
lot. That's what Browns fans have in common."
—*Laura Hlebak*

"I remember that my friend Tracy and I were coming home from a Pittsburgh game and the bone
blew off my BoneMobile and across the Shoreway.
It has been through snow storms, thunderstorms,
tornados, wind and more in the trips back and forth
. . . so the bone flies off and my friend Tracy sticks
her head out the window to look, and starts laughing. We couldn't pull off the Shoreway at the time,
but we went back to retrieve it later. When we told
everyone the following game what had happened, I

remember Scott [Nunnari] the BusDeacon and Bruce ["Datamigo" MacLaren] offered to replace it for free. Scott says to me, 'If you need help, we can fix that for you. They made me a bone a far better than the one then I had before—and they did it for nothing. Those are the kind of friends you make tailgating."
—***The BoneLady, superfan from Lakewood***

"The time flies. I remember after tailgating, we all used to sit behind home plate in the upper deck during Browns games. When the beer guys used to walk around [Municipal Stadium] with cases of beer, they'd dread hiking up the aisle to see us. They never wanted to come up, but we'd buy a whole case from them. Then they came up every time we needed to buy a round! Just this past year, when we played Miami and we were winning at halftime, I said to one of my buddies, 'I remember this same thing happened not too long ago.' And one of them said back to me, 'I don't know, Jim. I think Marino was the QB, and that was back in '86-'87.' Funny how that time gets past you." —***Jim Sgro, Parma***

Joe knows tailgating:
Think you're the Tailgate King? Here's a stat to make you feel inferior: In 2005 alone, Cahn traveled more than 35,000 miles in his deluxe, forty-foot Country Coach—nicknamed the "JoeMobile IV"—and tailgated at more than forty-five collegiate and NFL football games that year. He's been on his Tailgating America Tour since 1998, used over 80,000 gallons of fuel and has visited all 31 NFL stadiums, more than 120 college stadiums, and several NASCAR tracks.

"Back at the old [Municipal] Stadium, I remember hearing a tale from some of the security guys after the old Dawg Pound really took off. For a while, a bunch of fans and tailgaters would bring in this giant dog house. It was like a five-by-six foot house and took four or five guys to carry it into the Stadium. I guess the security people caught on after several weeks when there was only one guy carrying it out at the end of the game. That next week, security happened to look inside and found a keg of beer. These guys were bringing in a keg every week and emptying it during the game!" —*Tony Rizzo*

One fan remembers the best and worst and weather and crazy . . . all wrapped up into one:

"For me, it was that Oakland Raiders playoff game in 1981, the 'Red Right 88' game. I actually wasn't going to go down at all. I was working in a barber-shop in Cleveland Heights at the time and it was a bad weather week already. It was cold, the wind was blowing—zero [degree] weather the whole week. So this guy walks into the shop and asks if I wanted a couple tickets. I didn't think so, but he said 'Oh, take them anyway . . . you might change your mind.' I went down with my cousin and we stopped at Isa-bella Bakery at 69th and Detroit on the way down. They were pulling some pizzas out of the oven and we bought a dozen of them, wrapped them in alu-minum foil and thought we'd eat some before the game and sell the rest at halftime to people. By halftime, they were frozen! We were laughing, yell-ing to people 'Frozen pizzas here!' You know, that end zone interception happened right in front of us that day, which was a downer. Leaving the Stadium

was like going to a funeral. We've gone to a lot of funerals down there, you know? . . . I don't think the pizzas made it home. Maybe the Raiders ate them!"
—*Jim Sgro*

"A couple years ago, I took a friend with me to a game and I would always put my key to the BoneMobile in my pocket beforehand. We went to the game and coming out of the stadium, I reached in my pocket and my keys were gone. I could not find them anywhere. I ended up talking a cab home looking for the spare set of keys, but couldn't find them, so my brother [drove] me back to the Muni Lot without keys. I'm sitting in the lot—which looks like a war zone after a game—and thought 'There's no way I'm ever going to find the keys in this mess.' It was like a *Seinfeld* episode. So, we call a locksmith who takes like two hours to find us, charges me $100 to get into the car—which was all I happened to be carrying that day—and he is going to have to make me a key, which is going to cost extra. And at that moment, I happened to glance over at the windshield, and someone had tucked the keys under the wipers. I couldn't believe it. I thought they were gone forever! It was such a relief . . . and wouldn't you know that the next game, this guy came up to me and asked, 'Did you get your keys?' I asked him how he knew it was mine and he said, 'Well, you have the only Volvo in the parking lot!'"
—*The BoneLady*

Leave it to Cleveland's "Minister of Culture," Michael Heaton, to have his own story, which he's more than happy to share with tailgaters who might know a thing or two about Reverse Tailgating. Read on:

"Champs" by Michael Heaton

My story involves what I call Reverse Tailgating.

That means you stay downtown long after a Browns game has ended.

It was 1982 or '83. I was living in NYC and came back to Cleveland for a Browns /Jets game because I was meeting two old KSU college housemates, Kim Kristensen and Denis O*Keefe. Kim was still in Cleveland, Denis was in from D.C. In our usual disorganized fashion we had the meet-up mixed up. Was it Gate A? The Will Call window? For reasons still unknown—this was The Time Before Cell Phones—we never hooked up. It was a great game, the Browns won and on my way out I ran into *Plain Dealer* sportswriter Dennis Lustig.

I had known Dennis my whole life. He had worked with my dad. I got to know him better when I worked in the sports department myself, answering the *PD* Sportsline giving college scores to bookies. Did I mention Dennis was a dwarf?

Dennis was a dwarf.

Dennis was about three-foot-five and always needed a ride anywhere he was going. He also enjoyed cocktails after work. I was headed to the 2300 Club over on Payne Avenue to wet my whistle. Dennis was happy to ride along.

My drink back then was Stroh's with shots of Canadian Mist. Dennis had no problem with that program. The Browns must have won in a squeaker because we were happy and hit it pretty hard. Other *PD* sportswriters came in after their deadlines. It was a pretty good party.

When I went to collect my things, there was Dennis at the bar, O-U-T. He was long gone. I didn't know what to do with him. This was out of the range of my experience. What's the protocol for handling a dead-drunk dwarf? The bartender gave me his guidelines, and he knew Dennis well.

"You don't have to take him home, but you can't leave him here," he said pushing a piece of paper with Dennis' address on it across the bar to me.

I carried Dennis and his briefcase out to my car and put him in my backseat lying down. I knew how to get to Shaker Heights where Dennis lived with his mom like I knew Uzbekistan—meaning not that much. I decided to take him home. For safekeeping.

As I drove past Public Square, I couldn't believe my good fortune: there was one Yellow Cab there idling. I pulled a crazy u-turn, honking and flashing my lights. I put my car in park and opened the back door of the cab. Inside were two older businessmen in suits and raincoats.

"Going east?" I asked.

"Get in," they said.

"One minute," I answered.

When I returned they looked startled as I laid Dennis across their laps and put his briefcase in the front seat next to the driver.

I handed the driver the address from the bartender.

"Thanks. You guys are champs," I said.

And they were.

The Move: What Tailgaters Did to Pass the Time . . . and How They Helped Bring the Browns Back

The unthinkable happens. Browns fans reel from the ultimate gut-check sucker punch—the loss of *their team*—as owner Art Modell announces he's going to move his economically unviable team to Baltimore. We all know the story by now, but as a fan of the Browns, everyone knows you can't just shut that dedication off like a faucet or light switch. Faced with the prospect of no more NFL football for (at best) years or (at worst) ever, Browns tailgating fans shook off the daze, collected themselves and attempted to go on:

> "I was devastated when they news came that the team was moving. I remember the *Plain Dealer* calling me up and asking me about it. I took off work

for a while and spent time faxing letters to every NFL owner, congresspeople and league officials about why the Browns shouldn't move. I'm sure we broke some fax machines along the way. A group of Browns Backers had collected 1.5 million signatures and I went to Atlanta NFL owner's meeting with Dawn Brochetti, "Big Dawg" and others. We had three busloads of fans and tailgaters down there. And I think that made a statement." —*Tony "Mobile Dawg" Schaefer*

No lumps of coal for them! It's Christmastime with the Cleveland Believers, who gather around their light beer-inspired tree in the Muni Lot. *(Peter Chakerian)*

"When the Browns were gone, I was in college and had friends from the Rochester, New York area. One guy's dad was a Buffalo Bills season ticket holder. I had never been to another one of those stadiums for an NFL game. I think we were there for a Bills/New Orleans Saints game during Ricky Williams' rookie season. We got to Rich Stadium around 7:30 a.m. and partied all day. But when you lose your team, you don't know how to tailgate anymore! It was a rough ride back, but I remember before we left we were watching [quarterback] Doug Flutie—because he had left Buffalo by then—on a TV in the parking lot with other tailgaters there. Everyone there was watching him make his first start away from the Bills. Going home, I remember thinking that it really sucked not to have a team in Cleveland. You felt jealous that another team and the other fans were getting to have that

TailGator and tailgater partying it up in the Muni Lot. *(Karl Hassel)*

whole day's experience. I remember thinking, 'That's what we used to do.' Until then, missing the team was sort of an abstract experience—I don't think it sank in until that day, when I tailgated at another stadium. That's when it really hit me hard that the Browns were gone. I hated that feeling."
—Andre Knott, WTAM 1100 Browns beat reporter

"I heard stories about fans from the Muni Lot becoming fans of other teams when the Browns left, and I honestly just didn't get that. I still don't. If the team never came back, I was not going to watch the NFL ever again. That whole thing was like getting your heart ripped out. I love the game of football, it is my favorite game by far. In its pure form, it's the best. But when the business gets in the way, football is just not the same." **—The BoneLady**

"It ripped my heart out when the team moved. I was extremely bummed out when the Browns left. Honestly, it was hard for me to watch any football at all. I really couldn't tailgate anywhere else either; it just didn't feel right. I played a lot of golf instead. That next year, I knew a few people I worked with who started saying they were Steelers fans; I said to them, 'Good for you.' I never understood that."
—John Schoger

"I remember going up to Buffalo one year when the Browns weren't around—they used to have those 'Browns Fans Days' and a special section and tickets for all of us while the team was gone. I remember we brought a ton of Lake Erie perch to cook up, but they were frozen solid and we had to keep the bus running to thaw them out because it was so cold.

We did Buffalo for three years and tailgated there with a lot of Browns fans. The Buffalo Bills organization and their fans really treated us well up there."
—*Tony "Mobile Dawg" Schaefer*

"Over the years, [tailgating] really became a ritual. I didn't realize just what a great ritual it really was until the team left. We were all left feeling sort of blank."
—*Andre Knott*

The Return: Frustration

Just because the Cleveland Browns returned to the field in 1999, all wasn't necessarily right in the world. By now, Cleveland sports fans know that nothing about being a fan here is easy. It took close to a decade before the team began to look competent as a contender again. It's the kind of thing that one female fan I met during the 2007 season opener against the Pittsburgh Steelers likened to a bad relationship.

"You want to leave, but in the back of your mind you're always hopeful that things are going to change," she said, wishing to remain anonymous. "That's why we all keep coming back. No matter how many times we get our hearts broken, we still love the Browns and will always come back to them. It's not exactly a *healthy* relationship, as anyone with half a brain in their head—especially female—will tell you. But it is what it is, ya know? We love them and there's no way we'll leave them, even though we've all been tempted at one time or another."

Do other tailgating fans share the sentiment? What were the tailgating lots (and the fans there) like with the return of the team? Read on:

"The remarkable thing about the fans is how they continued to support the Browns in the mid-'90s, even after they were a lame duck team with a coach they hated [Bill Belichick] and a quarterback they despised [Vinnie Testaverde]. And they did the same when the team came back as well. But it was always much bigger than football, and I think the people were hanging on to that family thing as they do all over the Midwest. Football plays a huge part in holding Cleveland—and this part of the country— together. It's the same in Detroit and Buffalo and Pittsburgh. Football transcends its existence as a sport in the Midwest." —*Terry Pluto*

"For the last few years, we've been let down a lot. I can remember wondering if some of the fans were going to be coming back, because of how bad we were doing. At the beginning of the year, everyone is pumped up and ready to rock and roll because it's early in the season. But you'll see a trailing off when the team comes up short. In those seasons, by December, you're really left with the hardcore fans. Last year, that 2007 season, was different because we were winning. The Muni Lot was packed the entire time." —*Tony "Mobile Dawg" Schaefer*

"[The fan passion] reminds me of the NBA's Portland Trail Blazers, who are the only professional sports team in Portland, Oregon. You'll see Browns fans hang on to those player jerseys—Eric Turner, Kelly Holcomb, [Charlie] Frye, [Tim] Couch. Even if the player is obscure and played for ten minutes, or didn't do very well in Cleveland . . . if you're a former player you're almost a part of this 'royal family.' You're a part of the court, even if you're not necessarily the king. People like Al 'Bubba' Baker and Dick Ambrose will tell you that because of that, [Cleveland] is a place to really stay. The general tone and intelligence of Browns fans is pretty savvy. Cleveland is a town that understands you need linemen on the team and that it's not always as fun or sexy as a big name player. But that certainly says something good about the fans." —*Terry Pluto*

"Being around the Browns players, knowing them and listening to them, there is a huge respect for the fans who tailgate. Guys like [defensive lineman] Shaun Smith and [offensive guard] Eric Steinbach and I have traveled to stadiums together. Every time we've gone to a city like Baltimore or Pittsburgh, where you get the heat from the opposing team's tailgaters and you see the ones who have traveled to the game, it's gets to them every time . . . What's cool is that every player understands [the tailgating fan], and that pumps them up. There's always a sense that 'They're up early and getting ready for what we're getting ready for.' That's a lifeline for the

Headed in from Muni *(Charles Burkett Jr.)*

players. The players definitely recognize it. Trust me, they do." —*Andre Knott*

"My motto is, 'Thank God for Tailgating!' When you win two games all season, sometimes it's all you've got. All of what you see in the Muni Lot has happened since the team sucked. Imagine what it will be like when we are winners! You're starting to see shades of that now, since the team has improved. That first Pittsburgh game of 2007 was unbelievable and really telling. Last year's draft [of Joe Thomas and Brady Quinn] saved a lot of fans . . . and now that the team is winning, tailgating is going to blow up with that renewed faith. That first home game, we all go there on faith. Football's the common denominator, but tailgating is so much more than just about football." —*The BoneLady*

"What impresses me the most about Browns tailgaters is that even when our team sucked, they were all still there. Tailgating was the event and the Browns game was almost secondary—especially in '99, when the team came back. I've been covering the Browns since 1986, and spent some time in the Muni Lot. We've had camera crews in the Muni Lot when I did the *Sunday Sports Page* show with John Telich—and I'm always awed by the extravagance of the food and the set-ups that people have—but I've never been able to actually do it. I can't exactly booze it up and then head up to the press box, ya know?" —*Tony Rizzo*

"It's not to say that families are perfect, but when you have conflict in generations that happen—that rebelling against mom and dad, or generational

tension—all of that gets put aside for that Sunday afternoon. For that time, they are talking about other Browns games, ripping [Bill] Belichick and Art Modell, remembering Brian Sipe and Bernie Kosar . . . and maybe the younger kids are making a case for Braylon Edwards being the best Browns receiver ever. Those moments seem to be a real salve to put on those [relational] wounds. Bishop Joey Johnson [senior pastor of The House of the Lord in Akron] says that 'Even the best families have a lot of mess.' And sports helps to clean up some of that mess."
—*Terry Pluto*

"Thinking about tailgating now is funny for me, because I haven't done it in a long time. I'm still very fond of it, and jealous of my friends who do to a certain extent. With the job I do, my life has changed a lot. I still get the calls from my friends saying 'Hey, stop down to the Muni Lot,' but I rarely do. But when I drive downtown on the morning of a game, there's always that tug—that feeling of wanting to socialize and be a part of the gathering. A lot of people look at [tailgating] like it's just a bunch of drunks who are there. But it's not. If you don't get the culture, you don't get the culture. If you do, you love it. At the end of the day, tailgaters are a bunch of really passionate people and you don't get it unless you've been there and done it yourself." **—*Andre Knott***

Have a favorite tailgating experiences?
Share your story at:
www.brownstailgate.wordpress.com

ACKNOWLEDGMENTS

This book would not have been possible without the help, support, and guidance of Tony Acerno, Elisha Adams, Steven Batten, Gail Ghetia Bellamy, John Stark Bellamy II and Laura Serafin, Venechor Boyd, Dawn and Gary Brochetti, Eric Broder, Capt. Billy Buehl, Mary Kay Cabot, Joe "The Commissioner" Cahn, George Carr, Bruce Chamberlain, T.L. Champion, Mike Cipalla, Cleveland Public Library, Cleveland State University Library, Karen Cook and Terry Provost, Dan Coughlin, Ray Davis, Greg Deegan, Denny, Heather Dicks, Bob Dollinger, Kami Dolney, Josh Donald and Callie Scott, Eric and Cynthia Eakin, Matt Edwards, John Ettorre, Steve Fedorko, Kelly Ferjutz, Mark Fielder, Michael Gallucci, Glenn Gamboa, Anthony Garrison and the Phoenix/ Southwest Browns Backers for their hospitality, The Gecewich Family, Bob Geiger, Aaron Goldhammer, John Gorman, Kymberli Hagelberg, Kristin Hampshire, John "Radio" Hannibal, Mark Holan, Scott Huler, Rob Humphries, Bridget Huzicka, Kevin Keane, Bob Keesecker, Jennifer Keirn, Steve King, Don Kriss, Wayne Lett and the folks at Browns 24/7, Steven Liss, Scott Longert, Janet Macoska, Packy Malley, The Massoli Tribe and The Arborvitae Twelve, Colin McFarlane, Dan Moulthrop, Teri Mengert, The Morning Mafia, Vern Morrison, Linda and Fred Moss, Brian Motts, "Muni," Michael Norman, Scott Nunnari, Donal O'Shaughnessy, Eric Olsen, Daniel Ray Pickerel, Terry Pluto, Bill Reiter, Tony Rizzo, Karen Robinson, Josh Sabo, Angel Saurazas, Joseph Sheppa, Mike Stockdale, Jim Szatkowski, "Superfan" (who *never* answered his phone!), "The Taj," Claudia J. Taller, Paul Tepley, Elmer Turner, Vince Ventura, The Wenger Family, Chuck Yarborough, Chris Young and Jarrod Zickefoose.

Very special thanks to Layne Anderson, Mark "Munch" Bishop, Charles Burkett Jr., Michael, Monica and Will Chakerian, Pete and Ruth Chakerian, Randy Clevenger, Debra Darnall, The Giffords, Lance and Mary Beth Healy, Luke and Kate Healy, Michael Heaton, Laura Hlebak and Brian Leitch, Joy and Chris Klein, Andre Knott, Melanie Long, Emanual McElwain, Joe McElwain, JoEllen and Patrick McNamara, Thomas Mulready and Carol Hunt, George Nemeth and McKala Everett, Walter Novak, Mike Randall, Sandbridge Breakfast Club, Tony Schaefer, John Schoger, Jim Sgro, Mike and Laurie Smith, and Carlo Wolff and Karen Sandstrom. Props to "Diggit," "Monkeyman," "Punch the Clown," "Bandannie," and "C-Nek" for keeping it real.

A great big touchdown and two-point conversion to David Gray and the entire staff at Gray & Company for their confidence and support in this project.

I would also like to thank all the Cleveland Browns tailgating fans across the country who befriended me during the research of this book. I only wish I could have included every single one of you. By opening up your hearts, minds and lives—not even to mention your coolers, grills and vehicles!—I am truly humbled, grateful for your hospitality, insight and passion. There might be a team on the field with a claim on the name, but *YOU* are the Cleveland Browns. Don't let anybody tell you otherwise. See you in the lots!

And last (but definitely not least), to Susan and Christopher— this book wouldn't have been possible without your love and support. Thanks for helping me get into the end zone.

Layne Anderson

SOURCES

43 Places Stadium Page: http://www.43places.com/places/view/212623/
cleveland-browns-stadium-northcoast-harbor-cleveland
"A little sniffle, but no Browns Fever" —*Plain Dealer*, 1/05/2003: http://www.
psychologyofsports.com/guest/brownfever.htm
"A True-blue Brown" —Canton *Repository*, 6/30/2005: http://
www.cantonrep.com/topFive.php?vote=4&Headline=A+true-
blue+Brown&ID=230271&Category=11
Beerbelly and the Winerack: http://www.thebeerbelly.com
BigBlueTailgate.com: http://www.bigbluetailgate.com/tailgating_facts.html
BoneLady: http://www.bonelady.com
Braylon Bunch: http://www.braylonbunch.com
Browns 24/7: http://www.browns247.com
Browns Backers: http://www.brownsbacker.com
BusDeacon, Owner of DumDog Party Bus: http://www.myspace.com/busdeacon
Joe Cahn, Commissioner of Tailgating: http://www.tailgating.com
Charles Burkett Jr.'s Browns Photo Site: http://clevelandtailgate.blogspot.com
Cleveland Browns Official Site: http://www.clevelandbrowns.com
Cleveland Browns Bus: http://www.clevelandbrownsbus.com
Cleveland Stadium: The Last Chapter by Jim Toman, Gregory G. Deegan and
James A. Toman. Cleveland Landmarks Press
DJ Rezinate: http://www.myspace.com/rezinatemusic
Dawg Pound Mike: http://www.dawgpoundmike.com
Dawg Bones: http://www.dawgbones.com
Dawg Talk Island: http://www.dawgtalkisland.com
ESPN: The State of the NFL 2007: http://sports.espn.go.com/nfl/playoffs07/
news/story?id=3224311
ESPN Travel Pittsburgh: http://sports.espn.go.com/travel/news/
story?id=3118977
ESPN Travel Cincinnati: http://sports.espn.go.com/travel/news/
story?id=3007242
ESPN Travel Baltimore: http://sports.espn.go.com/travel/news/
story?id=3130455
"Euclid Couple Tackles Challenge" —The *News Herald*, 9/8/2007: http://
www.cantonrep.com/topFive.php?vote=4&Headline=A+true-
blue+Brown&ID=230271&Category=11
eVite Drink Calculator: http://www.evite.com/pages/party/drink-calculator.jsp
Feast Magazine: "Game Day Grub and Ed Rocheck's Tailgate Prep Guide":
http://www.thebrownsboard.com/images1/Feast%20Magazine%20
with%20Chef%20Ed.jpg http://www.feastmagazine.net
"Getting their game on: Die-hard Browns fans know regular season means big
party plays" —*Plain Dealer*, 9/7/2007
Giant Tower Game: http://www.mastersgames.com/cat/giant/giant-bricks.htm
Hammacher Schlemmer: http://www.hammacher.com
HighTechTailgating: http://www.hightechtailgating.com

Homeland Bunch Browns Backers: http://www.myspace.com/bunchbrowns-backers

JohnnyRoadTrip.com's Cleveland Tailgate Page: http://www.johnnyroadtrip.com/cities/cleveland/tailgating.htm

JohnnyRoadTrip's Baltimore Tailgate Page: http://www.johnnyroadtrip.com/cities/baltimore/tailgating.htm

JohnnyRoadTrip's Pittsburgh Tailgate Page: http://www.johnnyroadtrip.com/cities/pittsburgh/tailgating.htm

JohnnyRoadTrip's Cincinnati Tailgate Page:

http://www.johnnyroadtrip.com/cities/cincinnati/tailgating.htm

Lake Erie Islands Browns Backers: http://www.brownsbackersputinbay.com

Maximum Tailgating: http://www.maximumtailgating.com

Muni Lot Browns Backers http://www.munilotbrownsbackers.com

Muni Lot Mafia: http://www.munilotmafia.com

Muni the Lot Ness Monster: http://www.myspace.com/munithelotmonster

National Football League: http://www.nfl.com

NationalTailgate.com: http://www.nationaltailgate.com

"All Star Chefs Go the Extra Yard for Tailgating" — *The New York Times*, 9/28/2005:

http://www.nytimes.com/2005/09/28/dining/28tail.html?_r=1&8hpib&oref=slogin

"Cold Beer, Warm Grill and 80,000 of Your Closest Friends" — *The New York Times*, 10/25/2002:

http://query.nytimes.com/gst/fullpage.html?sec=travel&res=9B02E5D8133CF936A15753C1A9649C8B63

"Pro Football: The Price of Cleveland's Heart" — *The New York Times*, 9/2/1998: http://query.nytimes.com/gst/fullpage.html?res=9F01E1D6123FF931A3575AC0A96E958260&sec=&spon=&pagewanted=3

NPR: "For Chiefs Fans, Tailgating is not a Game": http://www.npr.org/templates/story/story.php?storyId=14589841

NPR: "The Real Truth About Men and Tailgating": http://www.npr.org/templates/story/story.php?storyId=4155655

TailgateDawg.com: http://www.tailgatedawg.com

The Browns Board Tailgate Page: http://www.thebrownsboard.com/tailgate.htm

The Browns Board Tailgate Party Page: http://www.thebrownsboard.com/Tailgate%20Party%20Q&A.html

The Browns List: http://www.brownslist.com

The Orange and Brown Report: http://www.cle.scout.com

"Magic Bus—Meet the Right Reverend Nunnari and his traveling bar" —*Scene* magazine, 10/10/04

Serious Fans: Browns Edition http://www.seriousfans.org

Southwest Browns Backers (Phoenix, AZ): http://www.brownsfanclub.com

Sportsnutz Browns Page: http://www.sportznutz.com/nfl/cle

Sports Illustrated: The Fan Value Experience: http://sportsillustrated.cnn.com/2007/football/nfl/11/01/fvi.intro/index.html

Tailgate Ideas: http://www.tailgatingideas.com

Tailgating Tips: http://cfc.wset.com/articles/getarticle.cfm?id=62

Viking Blogspot: Tailgating Statistics: http://vikingstailgate.blogspot.com/2007/10/mookie-quoted-in-star-tribune-story-on.html

Your Tailgate Party: http://www.yourtailgateparty.com

ABOUT THE AUTHOR

Peter Chakerian is an award-winning writer, reporter and journalist. His byline has appeared in the *Plain Dealer*, the *Akron Beacon Journal, Sun Newspapers, Cleveland Magazine, Northern Ohio Live, Scene, Cleveland Free Times, America Online, Blogcritics.org*, and dozens of other publications throughout the Midwest. He is the managing editor of CoolCleveland.com, a weekly online "e-blast" newsletter on arts, culture, economic development and all things cool in Cleveland. A lifelong northeast Ohio resident, a Cleveland State University graduate, and a Browns fan, he lives in Bay Village, Ohio with his wife, Susan, and son, Christopher.

Comments?

Want to share your comments, photos, and tailgating stories? Email me at clevelandbrownstailgate@yahoo.com. Visit and contribute to the *Browns Fan's Tailgating Guide* blog at **www.brownstailgate.wordpress.com**, which will be updated throughout the Cleveland Browns season.

Here we go, Brownies . . . here we go!

More good books about Cleveland and Ohio . . .

SPORTS - FOOTBALL

Browns Scrapbook / Memoirs of a Hall of Fame sportswriter looking back on five decades of Cleveland football. *Chuck Heaton* / $14.95 softcover

Browns Town 1964 / The remarkable story of the upstart AFC Cleveland Browns' surprise championship win over the hugely favored Baltimore Colts. *Terry Pluto* / $14.95 softcover

Heart of a Mule / Former Browns and OSU Buckeye player, Dick Schafrath retells many wild and entertaining stories from his life. *Dick Schafrath* / $24.95 hardcover

The Toe / No one played longer for the Browns. Relive the golden era of pro football in this autobiography by Lou "The Toe" Groza. *with Mark Hodermarsky* / $12.95 softcover

On Being Brown / Thoughtful and humorous essays and interviews with legendary Browns players ponder what it means to be a true Browns fan. *Scott Huler* / $12.95 softcover

False Start / A top sports journalist takes a hard look at the new Browns franchise and tells how it was set up to fail. *Terry Pluto* / $19.95 hardcover

SPORTS - BASEBALL

Dealing / A behind-the-scenes look at the Cleveland Indians front office that tells how and why trades and other deals are made to build the team. *Terry Pluto* / $14.95 softcover

The Top 20 Moments in Cleveland Sports Twenty exciting stories recount the most memorable and sensational events in Cleveland sports history. *Bob Dyer* / $14.95 softcover

Ask Hal / Answers to fans' most interesting questions about baseball rules from a Hall of Fame sportswriter. *Hal Lebovitz* / $14.95 softcover

The Curse of Rocky Colavito / The classic book about the Cleveland Indians' amazing era of futility: 1960-1993. *Terry Pluto* / $14.95 softcover

Whatever Happened to "Super Joe"? / Catch up with 45 good old guys from the bad old days of the Cleveland Indians. *Russell Schneider* / $14.95 softcover

Our Tribe / A father, a son, and the relationship they shared through their mutual devotion to the Cleveland Indians. *Terry Pluto* / $14.95 softcover

Omar! / All-Star shortstop Omar Vizquel retells his life story on and off the field in this candid baseball memoir. Includes 41 color photos. *With Bob Dyer* / $14.95 softcover

SPORTS - GENERAL

The Franchise / An in-depth look at how the Cleveland Cavaliers were completely rebuilt around superstar LeBron James. *Terry Pluto & Brian Windhorst* / $19.95 hardcover

Best of Hal Lebovitz / A collection of great sportswriting from six decades, by the late dean of Cleveland sportswriters. *Hal Lebovitz* / $14.95 softcover

Curses! Why Cleveland Sports Fans Deserve to Be Miserable / A collection of a lifetime of tough luck, bad breaks, goofs, and blunders. *Tim Long* / $9.95 softcover

LeBron James: The Rise of a Star / From high school hoops to #1 NBA draft pick, an inside look at the life and early career of basketball's hottest young star. *David Lee Morgan Jr.* / $14.95 softcover

Heroes, Scamps & Good Guys / 101 profiles of the most colorful characters from Cleveland sports history. Will rekindle memories for any Cleveland sports fan. *Bob Dolgan* / $24.95 hardcover

The View from Pluto / Award-winning sportswriter Terry Pluto's best columns about Northeast Ohio sports from 1990–2002. *Terry Pluto* / $14.95 softcover

Cleveland Golfer's Bible / All of Greater Cleveland's golf courses and driving ranges described in detail. Essential guide for any golfer. *John H. Tidyman* / $13.95 softcover

HISTORY & NOSTALGIA

The Buzzard / A rock and roll radio memoir about the wild days at Cleveland's WMMS from 1973 to 1986. *John Gorman* / $14.95 softcover

Cleveland Rock & Roll Memories / Revisit the glory days of rock & roll in Cleveland. *Carlo Wolff* / $19.95 softcover

Strange Tales from Ohio / Offbeat tales about the Buckeye State's most remarkable people, places, and events. *Neil Zurcher* / $13.95 softcover

Cemeteries of Northeast Ohio / Meet our most interesting "permanent residents" at 120 local cemeteries. *Vicki Blum Vigil* / $15.95 softcover

Cleveland Food Memories / A nostalgic look back at the food we loved, the places we bought it, and the people who made it special. *Gail Ghetia Bellamy* / $17.95 softcover

Cleveland Amusement Park Memories A nostalgic look back at Euclid Beach Park, Puritas Springs Park, Geauga Lake Park, and other classic parks. *David & Diane Francis* / $19.95 softcover

Barnaby and Me / Linn Sheldon, a Cleveland TV legend as "Barnaby," tells the fascinating story of his own extraordinary life. / $12.95 softcover

The Cleveland Orchestra Story / How a midwestern orchestra became a titan in the world of classical music. With 102 rare photographs. *Donald Rosenberg* / $40.00 hardcover

Ghoulardi / The behind-the-scenes story of Cleveland's wildest TV legend. Rare photos, interviews, show transcripts, and Ghoulardi trivia. *Tom Feran & R. D. Heldenfels* / $17.95 softcover

Whatever Happened to the "Paper Rex" Man? / Nostalgic essays and photos rekindle memories of Cleveland's Near West Side neighborhood. *The May Dugan Center* / $15.95 softcover

NATURE & OUTDOORS

Cleveland on Foot / Beyond Cleveland on Foot / Great hikes and self-guided walking tours in and around Greater Cleveland and 7 neighboring counties. *Patience Cameron Hoskins, with Rob & Peg Bobel* / $15.95 (each) softcover

Trail Guide to Cuyahoga Valley National Park / The complete guide to Ohio's own national park, written by the people who know it best. *Cuyahoga Valley Trails Council* / $15.95 softcover

Cleveland Fishing Guide / Best public fishing spots in Northeast Ohio, what kind of fish you'll find, and how to catch them. Directory of fishing resources. *John Barbo* / $14.95 softcover

Dick Goddard's Weather Guide for Northeast Ohio / Seasonal facts, folklore, storm tips, and weather from Cleveland's top meteorologist. / $13.95 softcover

TRAVEL & GUIDES

Ohio Road Trips / Discover 52 of Neil Zurcher's all-time favorite Ohio getaways. *Neil Zurcher* / $13.95 softcover

Cleveland Ethnic Eats / The guide to authentic ethnic restaurants and markets in Northeast Ohio. *Laura Taxel* / $13.95 softcover

52 Romantic Outings in Greater Cleveland / Easy-to-follow "recipes" for romance —a lunch hour, an evening, or a full day together. *Miriam Carey* / $13.95 softcover

Bed & Breakfast Getaways from Cleveland / Great Inn Getaways from Cleveland / Small inns and hotels, perfect for an easy weekend or evening away from home. *Doris Larson* / $14.95 (each) softcover

Ohio Oddities / An armchair guide to the offbeat, way out, wacky, oddball, and otherwise curious roadside attractions of the Buckeye State. *Neil Zurcher* / $13.95 softcover

CRIME & MYSTERY

Cleveland Cops / Sixty cops tell gritty and funny stories about patrolling the streets of Cleveland. *John H. Tidyman* / $14.95 paperback

Amy: My Search for Her Killer / Secrets and suspects in the unsolved murder of Amy Mihaljevic. *James Renner* / $24.95 hardcover

**They Died Crawling
The Maniac in the Bushes
The Corpse in the Cellar
The Killer in the Attic
Death Ride at Euclid Beach**
Five collections of gripping true tales about notable Cleveland crimes and disasters. Includes photos. *John Stark Bellamy II* / $13.95 softcover (each)

Women Behaving Badly / 16 strange-but-true tales of Cleveland's most ferocious female killers. *John Stark Bellamy II* / $24.95 hardcover

The Milan Jacovich mystery series / Cleveland's favorite private eye solves tough cases in these 13 popular detective novels. *Les Roberts* / $13.95 (each) softcover

King of the Holly Hop / #14 in the popular Milan Jacovich mystery series. *Les Roberts* / $24.95 hardcover

Available from your favorite bookseller.
More info at: **www.grayco.com**